CROSS ___DS

Better Choices for a Better Life

DAVID CERULLO

INSPIRATION
MINISTRIES

CROSSROADS
Better Choices for a Better Life

Published by
Inspiration Ministries
P.O. Box 7750
Charlotte, NC 28241

Printed in the United States of America

—— ◯◯ ——

DEDICATION

To the Friends and Partners of
Inspiration Ministries.

May these words help you
make the right choices in your life…
choices God will reward in this present life
AND in the life to come.

David

CONTENTS

"This is what the Lord says: 'Stand at the crossroads and look; ask for the ancient paths, ask where the good way is, and walk in it, and you will find rest for your souls.'"

— Jeremiah 6:16 NIV

INTRODUCTION

A S I BEGAN TO WRITE THIS BOOK, I sensed a great excitement about what God wants to do in your life. No matter what kind of crossroads you may be facing today—in your health, finances, career, or family—I'm convinced the Lord wants to give you a breakthrough.

Even if you you have felt "stuck" or defeated in some area of your life for many years, your turnaround can come amazingly quickly. Remember the woman who suffered from a hemorrhage for 12 years (Mark 5:25-34)? Or the man who was sick for 38 years before Jesus instantly healed him (John 5:2-9)?

Yet breakthroughs are never automatic. They require a decision on our part to believe God's promises and do what He tells us to do. This choice is stated clearly in Isaiah 1:19-20: *"If you consent and obey, you will eat the best of the land; but if you refuse and rebel, you will be devoured by the sword."*

Friend, I'm trusting today that you will *"consent and obey"* as God's Word is unveiled in this book. If so, you will be blessed!

A SOBERING REALITY

I'm fully aware that not everyone will decide to heed the message in this book. I've sensed the Lord impressing upon me, "David, there are three kinds of people who need this message."

First, the Lord said, "One category is those who are on the brink of making the worst choices they will ever make in their lives. They will regret the consequences of these decisions for eternity. But if they will stop right now and listen to Me, I will help them make the *right* choices."

Next, He told me, "There are others reading this message who are on the verge of making some of their *greatest* and most important decisions. If they will make the choices I am setting before them, I will reward them for taking a step of faith and obedience. I will open the windows of Heaven and pour out blessings upon them that will last throughout this life—and precede them into the life to come."

Finally, He said, "There is a third group of people who are bound with fear, doubt, and uncertainty—those who have vacillated from one decision to the next. I want these people to know that unless they begin to walk by faith and not by fear—unless they step out and make the right choices—they won't receive anything from Me."

Regardless of which of these categories you are in, I believe the Lord has placed this book into your hands for His divine purpose. He wants you to know that today, and every day of your life, you are making choices that affect your family, your finances, your health, your relationships, your spiritual life—plus much more. As we will discover, the decisions we make today not only have a dramatic impact during our life on earth, but also for eternity.

REWARDS AND CONSEQUENCES

As much as some people would like to avoid this subject, *every* choice we make—whether good or bad—has an unavoidable reward or consequences. It's like the law of physics: *For every action there is a reaction.*

From the beginning, God established principles by

which we are to live. Then He gives us a choice: We either can accept or reject His Word—obey or disobey. As sure as the sun will rise tomorrow, for each decision, there *IS* a consequence.

A LIFE-CHANGING JOURNEY

This book was written to change your life, not just to fill your head with empty facts. God's Word is powerful, and it's power is activated when we make a commitment to put it into *action* (James 1:22-25).

In the following chapters, I will share:

- How to make the most important choice of your life.
- What God says about blessings and curses.
- How your decisions will affect your reputation and relationships.
- Powerful choices that can defeat the devil.
- Ten steps to making wise choices.
- Choices that determine your destiny.

I pray that as a result of what you are about to read, you will understand the importance of even your *smallest* choices. May you gain new wisdom for making the *right* decisions—those that are in the very center of God's will.

I am thrilled we are taking this rewarding journey together. Your life will never be the same!

—David Cerullo

YOUR POWER TO CHOOSE

Between two evils
choose neither;
between two goods,
choose both.

TYRONE EDWARDS

Decisions! Decisions! Decisions! We make hundreds — even thousands of them — every day. Black sweater or blue? Coffee or tea? KFC or Taco Bell? Paper or plastic? Answer the phone or let it ring? Read my Bible now or wait until later? Drive the main road or take a shortcut? Listen to the news or some worship music?

Our routine choices may seem insignificant, yet all our decisions affect us in one way or another. Hidden in this constant drumbeat of decision-making are major turning points—options we take that become major chapters in our life story.

SHOULD I GRUMBLE AND COMPLAIN?

As a child, I was faced with a tough decision.

I thank the Lord that I am privileged to have a father who loves me — many don't. Yet, as I grew up, my father was gone most of the time. My dad, international evangelist Morris Cerullo, was called by God to preach the Gospel and build an army of ministers worldwide. As a result, he was away from home almost 300 days of the year. While other boys my age had their fathers around to watch them play baseball or football, my dad was somewhere in the four corners of the earth—Africa, Asia, South America, and beyond.

I had a choice to make. I could grumble, complain, and make life miserable for my parents, or I could willingly give my father to the nations of the world without murmuring. I chose to make that sacrifice.

In my early years, our family (I have a sister, Susan, living; and a brother, Mark, with the Lord) would journey together to Dad's crusades. When we reached school age, however, my parents decided that it was best for us to stay in one location and let him travel with his ministry team.

Whenever my father would take me with him to an overseas crusade, it was exciting to experience a foreign culture. Those trips made a lasting impression on me. Often I saw people's humble living conditions—the huts, the starvation, and the abject poverty. I also witnessed firsthand the spiritual starvation of hearts hungry for the Gospel.

Even then, I was making decisions pertaining to my future. When I saw the power of God open blind eyes, unstop deaf ears, and cause the lame to walk, the Lord began stirring something within me. At this young age, I was developing a heart for the Lost and a special compassion for the suffering.

A DOCTOR?

I began to pray, "Lord, I want to do something to make a difference in the world."

Not once did I feel drawn to become a preacher. Instead I thought, "If I could be a medical doctor, God could use me to help alleviate sickness and pain in people's lives." While other boys went through stages, dreaming of becoming a policeman one minute and a fireman the next, I always wanted to be a doctor.

For some reason, I constantly seemed to be in a hurry. I graduated from high school early and applied to the University of California at San Diego, which had a great medical school. I was on my way!

One small detail: As a teenager, I entered into what I thought was a serious "love interest" with a girl. We even talked marriage.

When my parents heard the news, they went ballistic!

As kindly as they could, they essentially said, "Son, you're crazy! What are you thinking? You're far too young. You have your whole life ahead of you!" And they added, "Most importantly, we don't feel this person is right for you spiritually."

I was devastated. My parents convinced me to go to school out of state to Oral Roberts University and "try it" for one semester. If I didn't like the school, I could come home and go to the University of California at San Diego. So at 17 years of age, I enrolled in the pre-med program at ORU and began to follow my dream.

Not long afterwards, in God's providence, I met a beautiful girl in Tulsa named Barbara, who three years later would become my wife. Suffice it to say, I wasn't going home to San Diego anytime soon!

GOD'S QUESTION

Two years into my college experience, while I was studying in my dorm room, God suddenly spoke to me: "David, what about My Kingdom?" Then He repeated the question. "David, what about My Kingdom?"

My response was, "What about it, Lord? I'm studying medicine. I'm going to be a doctor to help heal suffering humanity."

God continued asking, "What about My Kingdom?"

It became abundantly clear that the Lord had other plans for my life. He was asking me to lay down my planned career in medicine and make a different *choice* about my future. For as long as I could remember, I had wanted to be a physician, and now God was asking me to take another route.

I began praying, "Lord, if you want me to lay aside

medicine and follow you in ministry, I will." Even then, I didn't feel God leading me to be a minister in the traditional sense. Instead, I believed I was to change my college major to business, so I did.

You see, when I was growing up, Dad never talked to me about entering the ministry—or even working with him at some time in the future. But I felt that if I could help relieve the burden of the business and administration side of his worldwide outreach, he could be more effective in focusing on the ministry itself. I called my father and shared my decision with him.

I asked, "Dad, do you feel there is a place for me in your ministry in San Diego?"

"Of course there is!" he replied.

Again in a hurry (why, I don't know, but I always seemed to be in a hurry!), I changed majors and graduated one year early. Barbara and I were soon married, and off to San Diego we went.

The choices I made during those early years proved pivotal in the journey God had planned for our life and family.

CHANGE YOUR CHOICES!

I am excited about what God wants to do in your life as you read these pages. Why? Because I believe the message God has asked me to share with you is absolutely vital for you and those you love.

Years ago I heard these compelling words: *If you want to change your future, change your choices!*

Think about that statement for a moment. Do you realize how the decisions you make today impact everything about tomorrow? It's true! We are the sum total of our life choices—whether for good or bad. Better choices today will always lead to a better life tomorrow.

From the moment of creation, the Almighty gave His children an awesome, life-changing power—the power to choose. Instead of making us puppets with heavenly strings, He gave us a free will to make moral choices. We have the responsibility to choose between God or Satan, life or death, wisdom or folly, obedience or sin.

Not only will our decisions affect our future on earth, they will also determine *where*—and *how*—we will spend eternity.

2

CHOICES BRING REWARDS

Destiny is not a matter of chance,
it is a matter of choice:
it is not a thing to be waited for,
it is a thing to be achieved.

WILLIAM JENNINGS BRYAN

Have you ever stopped to think about how the choices you make in this life affect not only your future here on earth, but also your future in eternity? Your choices bring rewards. Choices bring consequences. The choices you make today determine your future.

God asks us all to make important choices. You make choices that affect your family, your future, and the "here and now," but you also make choices that very much affect the "there and then" of eternity.

You are the sum total of all the choices you've made in life from earliest childhood to where you are today. Where you are in life now—your job, your family, your present circumstances—are all a result of the choices you made from the crossroads God set before you. Choices always have consequences for good or for bad.

God's Word is full of promises, both rewards and consequences. In Leviticus 26, you'll find 40 verses of blessings and curses. The Lord said, *"If you walk in my statutes and keep my commandments and do them, **then** I will give you rain in due season. Then the land will yield its increase"* (vs. 3-4).

In Deuteronomy 28, there are 68 verses focusing on blessings and curses. The Lord says in His Word, *"It shall come to be, if you diligently obey the LORD your God, being careful to do all His commandments which I command you today...all these blessings will come upon you and overtake you if you obey the LORD your God"* (vs. 1-2).

It's interesting that the first 14 verses in Deuteronomy 28 tell of the blessings from God, but the next 53 verses speak about curses. For some reason, God uses nearly four times as many verses in this passage to talk about the curses He would bring upon us for making the wrong choices than He does in explaining the blessings we would receive from Him for making the right choices. Apparently, God is more interested in our understanding the consequences of making the wrong choice than He is in our understanding the consequences of making the right choice. Why? Why does God focus so much on the results of making *wrong* choices? My guess is that He wants us to think long and hard about the consequences of making wrong choices!

WHAT ABOUT TODAY?

God clearly sets before us choices and decisions to make. His Word says that if we obey Him and make the right choices, we will have a positive reward. And if we disobey Him and make the wrong choices, we will Reap curses instead. It's that simple.

I know "curses" is a strong word to use, but this is what the Bible says, not me. You may be reading this book and saying, "Well, wait a minute, David. The books of Leviticus and Deuteronomy are in the *Old Testament*. That was all the *Old Covenant*—written under the law. Today, God has given us a *New Testament*, a *New Covenant*. We live under grace now."

Of course, I believe this is true, but listen to what Deuteronomy 29 also says: *"Now, and not with you alone, am I making this covenant and this oath but with those who stand here with us today in the presence of the Lord our God **and with those who are not with us here today**"* (vs. 14-15).

Also listen to what the apostle Paul wrote in his first letter to the Corinthians: *"With many of them God was not well pleased for they were overthrown in the wilderness. Now these things were our examples"* (10:5). In the eleventh verse Paul says, *"All these things happened to them as an example to us."*

You know, I love grace, and I'm so thankful God renews His grace to us each and every day. But we can't keep running around as so many like to do saying, "Grace, grace, grace," and then use grace as a license to choose unwisely.

Paul asks in Romans 6:1-2: *"What shall we say then? Shall we continue in sin, that grace may abound? God forbid."* Where God's law was present in the Old Testament, there was also His *grace*; where you find grace in the New Testament, believe me, it is still hazardous to disregard God's *law*.

THE COMING HARVEST

Let's get back to choices. My friend, the most important choice God will ever ask you to make is to accept the gift of His Son Jesus Christ and make Him the Lord of your life. The consequences of *this* choice determine *where* you're going to spend eternity. But other choices you make in life, your behavior and actions—those choices and decisions unlock the door to God's rewards, and they determine *how* you're going to spend eternity.

The choices you make about the Seeds you Sow in this lifetime—Seeds of love, prayer, gentleness, kindness, giving—these Seeds produce a bountiful Harvest of rewards, now in this lifetime, and also in a Harvest of rewards that are waiting for you in eternity.

Sadly, many people don't stop to think about the consequences of the negative of Seeds they Sow—Seeds of anger, bitterness, harsh words, or gossip. These Seeds also bear Harvests, in this lifetime AND in eternity.

YOUR COMPENSATION

The Harvests of rewards you produce are a result of the Seeds you Sow. Jesus said in Matthew 16:27, *"The Son of Man is going to come in the glory of His Father with His angels and then **He will reward each according to his works."***

When most people think about rewards, they think about good things, positive things. A reward is something special, isn't it? Well, no. That's really a misinterpretation of the word "reward." A reward is simply compensation—something received in return for something done. A reward can be either good or bad.

Compensation really means to weigh one thing against another. Imagine for a moment the old-fashioned scales people used to weigh something. You would place what you wanted to weigh on one side of the scale and put a known weight on the other side. You weighed one thing against another. You were looking for an equivalent weight. Which is heavier? Which is lighter?

But what is the equivalent compensation in terms of the choices you make? It's the equivalent of what you *do.* Jesus says your rewards will be according, or equivalent, to your works.

Now, you may not consciously go though your day making choices based on a reward you expect to receive, thinking, "If I do *this,* God will reward me." Yet, your right choices will bring a lifetime of rewards, now in this life AND in the life to come.

There is another side to this. Wrong choices will result in a lifetime of pain, regret, and sorrow—not just in this life, but also in the life to come.

THE THREE "T'S"

Here are three things God gives each of us:

- **Time**—God gives each of us 24 hours a day, seven days a week.
- **Talent**—God gives each of us different talents and gifts.
- **Treasure**—God gives each of us different resources.

We all have the opportunity to invest what we have been given. It's *how* we choose to *Sow* our time...how we choose to *use* our talents...how we choose to *invest* the treasure He's given us that determine our rewards now.

I keep stressing eternity because I talk to so many people who just think about today. They live in, and for, the "now." But we have a life *after* "now," and it's a lot longer than "now," believe me!

We're finite human beings. We have little comprehension of time. Eternity is something we have a hard time understanding.

The Lord says that maybe we'll live three score and ten—that's 70 years. Or, if we're strong, maybe we'll live another ten years to age 80 (Psalm 90:10). But what is 80 years compared to the scope of eternity? It's not even a vapor or a blink of an eye.

Yet many people spend so much time making choices that affect them here and now, and they forget about the choices that are going to affect them there and then.

Jesus promises in Revelation 22:12 that He's coming again and that He's bringing *rewards* with Him to give to each person according to their works. 1 Corinthians 3:8 declares, *"Each will receive his own reward according to his own labor."* Revelation 20:13 says, *"They were judged every man according to their works."*

By now it should be very clear: *Where* you spend eternity depends on what you believe, but *how* you spend eternity depends on the choices you make—in this present life.

YOUR "WAGES"

What you do today affects not only the experiences you and your family will have in this lifetime, but the consequences will affect your life forever. Jesus has a lot to say about rewards. He taught in Luke 14 that we will be repaid at the resurrection of the just—that's after we have passed on from this life—for good deeds and works we've done.

He also said that our rewards come after we're in Heaven as a result of what we did here on earth. In Luke 6:23, Jesus said, *"Rejoice in that day and leap for joy for indeed your reward is great in heaven."*

When you translate the word "reward" that Jesus used in this passage, it means "wages." So, Jesus is saying your wages—what you've worked so hard to earn—are going to be great. His *repayment* will be in return for something you did.

Jesus used he same word in the story of the Good Samaritan in Luke 10:35. He said, *"I will repay you."* And it's the same word He used in Mark 9:41 when He said, *"Whoever gives a cup of water in my name will by no means lose his repayment."*

I love what the writer of the book of Hebrews states: *"Without faith it's impossible to please God for he who comes to God must believe that He is and that He is a **rewarder** of those who diligently seek Him"* (Hebrews 11:6). Yes, God is a Rewarder.

One day soon, we're going to stand in the presence of God, and He is going to present our "wages" for the choices and actions we took here on this earth, whether those choices had good or bad consequences.

God's divine scales will be placed before us. Our good choices are going to be stacked up on one side—the bad choices are going to be stacked up on the other side. Which way are the scales of *your* life going to tip?

A MANSION?

Jesus said, *"In my Father's house are many mansions— and I go to prepare a place for you"* (John 14:2). So many people have taken for granted that they have a mansion, as the song says, "just over the hilltop—in that bright land where I'll never grow old." However, I'm not so sure that we *all* have a mansion just over the hilltop, a palatial estate on the other side.

The *"place for you"* may be entirely different from what you expect. I encourage you to study the Word and see what He's really saying. What you are going to be "living in" in Heaven (the rewards you're going to receive) are going to be in response to the choices you made here on this earth—what you did with your time, your talent, and your treasure. It will not be the same for every person.

Pay close attention to how Paul describes what lies ahead: *"We must all appear before the judgment seat of Christ that each one may receive the things done in the body according to what he has done whether good or bad"* (2 Corinthians 5:10).

Paul doesn't say we're going to be judged on the basis of our beliefs. When you invited Jesus Christ into your life, you made a choice on *where* you would spend eternity. But Paul *did* say we're going to be judged and tested on the basis of our *works*. They are what determine the *level* of living we experience in Heaven.

SUFFERING LOSS IN ETERNITY?

If what you do with your life—the choices you make—endure as gold, silver, and precious stones, you will be positively rewarded. If, on the other hand, your choices amount to hay, wood, and stubble, guess what is going to happen? They will burn up, and there's going to be little or nothing left on that scale to reward (1 Corinthians 3:12-15).

To me, the sobering point of 1 Corinthians 3 is simply this: *"If anyone's work is burned, he's going to suffer loss."* You may ask, "How do you suffer loss in Heaven? Is this really possible? Isn't Heaven the *prize*? Isn't this the *hope*? Isn't that the *land* we're all trying to reach?"

Well, yes, but Paul makes it clear that it's possible to reach Heaven and still suffer loss. Loss of what? *Loss of the reward you might have received if only you had made the right choices.* If you made the wrong choices, your reward will be placed on a fire and burned up.

As we continue, it's so important to keep in mind that every choice we make brings a reward—both now in this lifetime AND in the world to come. So let's make the RIGHT choices!

3

AN EXAMPLE
TO US

*People seldom improve
when they have no other model
but themselves to copy.*

OLIVER GOLDSMITH

I encourage you to go through your Bible, starting at the beginning of Genesis and proceeding to the end of Revelation. Make a list of all the choices people made in the Bible and the consequences of those choices. Some made wise choices and received great rewards. Others made foolish choices and suffered as a result.

At every turn in God's Word—in the lives of Ruth, David, Solomon, Elisha, Daniel, Jonah, and so many more—we see the result of choices. Their lives and the choices they made are examples to us. The rewards they received—and the consequences of their bad choices—speak to us today.

Notice what the apostle Paul writes to the Believers at Corinth. Speaking of the children of Israel, he says, *"With most of them God was not well-pleased; for they were laid low in the wilderness"* (1 Corinthians 10:5). Then he adds, *"Now these things happened to them as an example, and they were written for our instruction"* (v. 11).

The experiences of those who have gone before us—their choices and rewards—are lessons for us today as we face our own crossroads and decisions.

THE FIRST CHOICE

We often forget that our very existence is the result of a choice by God. He desired to have a family on earth with whom He could have fellowship—that was His reward.

When God created Adam and Eve, He gave them a perfect world in which to live, and there was only one word of caution. The Lord instructed them: *"From any tree of the garden you may eat freely; but from the tree of the knowledge of good and evil you shall not eat, for in the day that you eat from it you will surely die"* (Genesis 2:16-17).

However, the first man and woman *chose* to disobey

God. As a result, sin, sickness, and death entered the world. Even more, man lost his direct fellowship with God.

"LORD, WHAT IS RAIN?"

In Genesis 6, the Lord commanded Noah to build an ark. What choice did Noah face? To obey or to disobey.

"Noah, it's going to rain," announced the Almighty.

"Rain, Lord? What's rain?" (Until that point in time, people had never seen rain. The Bible only describes a "mist" that covered the earth.)

"Noah, you're going to need to build an ark," the Lord instructed.

"What's an ark?" he likely asked.

Can you imagine this conversation taking place between *you* and God? Think about all your friends gathering around to watch what you were doing!

"What are you building?" his friends asked.

"An ark," replied Noah.

"Why?" they wanted to know.

"Because God said it's going to rain!"

"What's rain? What's an ark?" they inquired. "Noah, you're crazy!" they concluded.

For 120 years, Noah built the ark—despite the embarrassment. He chose to endure the ridicule and obey God, even though I'm sure he was bewildered at times.

What was his reward? What did he receive as the consequence of his choice to obey? Not only were Noah and his family saved from the flood, but the entire world was repopulated, and through his seed would come the Savior of the world!

Notice that the first action of Noah when he left the ark was to build an altar and offer a sacrifice (Genesis 8:20).

That decision produced an amazing reward. After God smelled the soothing aroma (the offering), He declared, *"I will never again curse the ground on account of man, for the intent of man's heart is evil from his youth; and I will never again destroy every living thing, as I have done"* (v. 21).

As a result of Noah's obedience, *and* as a direct consequence of his offerings, God blessed him abundantly (Genesis 9:7). The Lord also established His Covenant with him (v. 11).

I shudder to think what would have happened if Noah had not built an altar and offered a sacrifice. Would God have destroyed the earth with no survivors? Would He have started over here or on some other planet? Or not at all?

Today, perhaps the greatest thing we can do—both *during* a crisis and *after* one—is to *"offer the sacrifice of praise to God continually, that is, the fruit of our lips giving thanks to his name"* (Hebrews 13:15 KJV).

OBEDIENCE HAS ITS REWARDS

Are you beginning to see God's pattern? For every choice we make, there is a reward. And the reward is not always good—sometimes what we receive is an unwanted consequence.

The Lord told Abram, *"Go forth from your country, and from your relatives and from your father's house, to the land which I will show you; And I will make you a great nation, and I will bless you, and make your name great; And so you shall be a blessing; And I will bless those who bless you, and the one who curses you I will curse. And in you all the families of the earth will be blessed"* (Genesis 12:1-3).

Abram had a choice to make. He could stay where he was—or leave his home and trust God to bring His will to pass. Abram was faced with the choice of turning his back on everything that was comfortable and familiar—his home, his friends, his surroundings, and even his family. It was a huge step of faith!

Because he chose to respond to the voice of the Lord, God gave him—and his descendants—the land of promise and an incredible impact throughout history.

What would have been the consequences if Abram had not obeyed God? The Bible makes it clear that disobedience also produces negative rewards.

DON'T BE IMPATIENT

Since Abram and Sarah had no children, Sarah grew impatient with God and said to her husband, *"Now behold, the Lord has prevented me from bearing children. Please go in to my maid; perhaps I will obtain children through her"* (Genesis 16:2).

So if the Lord *prevented* Sarah from having children, why did she send Hagar to Abram? Sarah and Abram made a foolish and unwise choice...and they suffered the consequences of that choice.

They chose to do things their own way instead of according to God's plan, and the consequence was the birth of Ishmael. Even though he was not the "son of promise" God had spoken of, his seed was multiplied. Ishmael was the son born of impatience and disobedience.

What has been the outcome of Sarah and Abram's choice? For thousands of years, there has been strife, tension, and bloodshed in the Middle East as the sons of

Ishmael and the sons of Isaac have battled. The results of Abram and Sarah's wrong choice have gone far beyond the boundaries of their own family. Four thousand years later, this struggle encompasses not just Arab and Jew, but all mankind.

I agree with many Biblical scholars who believe the present conflict in the Middle East stems from Abram and Sarah's misguided choice. Ishmael's birth was not God's intention for them, nor for the world.

GREATER BLESSINGS!

Abram was 99 years old when the Lord once more appeared to him, saying, *"I am God Almighty; Walk before Me, and be blameless"* (Genesis 17:1). Even more, God made a covenant with him and changed his name to Abraham—the father of many nations (Genesis 17:5).

Despite their old age, God gave Abraham and Sarah a son, Isaac. The Lord established an everlasting covenant with Isaac and with his seed after him (v. 19). Still, the Lord was not finished with the testing of Abraham. God asked him to make a choice to obey Him and offer Isaac on the altar of sacrifice (Genesis 22).

You see, God had made a covenant with Abraham to bless him and make his children as numerous as the stars in the sky. Yet, in the face of this covenant promise, God asked Abraham to offer Isaac as a sacrifice. How could God's promise possibly come true if Abraham were to obey Him and offer Isaac as a sacrifice? Abraham didn't try to reason with God; instead he *chose* to believe God would somehow provide a sacrifice.

My friend, obedience is a *choice*. Because Abraham chose to obey, God intervened, saying: *"Do not stretch out*

*your hand against the lad, and do nothing to him; for now
I know that you fear God, since you have not withheld your
son, your only son, from Me"* (Genesis 22:12). Instead, the
Lord prepared a substitute—a ram to be slain on the altar
in place of Isaac.

Through this experience, God renewed His Covenant
with Abraham. Earlier, the Lord said He would bless him
and multiply his seed. Now God was declaring He would
greatly bless him: *"I will greatly bless you, and I will greatly
multiply your seed as the stars of the heavens and as the
sand which is on the seashore; and your seed shall possess
the gate of their enemies"* (Genesis 22:17).

Abraham received a *greater* reward because of his
choice to obey—and so can you!

TRIUMPH OR TRAVAIL?

As we are discovering, the decisions we make can have
a profound impact on our personal life, family, finances,
and so much more—both now and in eternity. That's why
I want you to see the "cause and effect" pattern God has
established for our choices—they result either in joy or in
sorrow, triumph, or travail.

Do you remember the story of Jacob wrestling with an
angel—probably God Himself? (Genesis 33). Jacob chose
not to give up, but to prevail. He would not let go until he
was blessed and received the answer to his heart's cry. As
a reward, God changed his name from Jacob to Israel.
Instead of just seeking the blessing, he *became* a blessing.
Jacob's walk and his talk were transformed. God changed
his entire destiny because he chose to prevail!

FEAR OR FAITH? YOU DECIDE

Think about Moses. Here was a man hand-picked by God to deliver His people out of their bondage in Egypt. What would have happened if Moses had refused to obey?

During their great Exodus out of Egypt, the children of Israel chose to grumble and complain in the wilderness, allowing fear to rule their hearts and tongues. Growing restless while waiting for Moses to come down from the mountain of God, they made a god of their own—a golden calf. Because they chose to corrupt themselves, they reaped a reward of punishment. The Bible records that 3,000 people died that day because of their disobedience (Exodus 32:28).

Again and again, God tested the children of Israel by offering them choices. Obedience brought blessing, health, provision, and victory in battle. Failure to follow God's direction resulted in punishment and loss.

THEY SAW GRASSHOPPERS

When the 12 spies were sent to Canaan for a firsthand look at the Promised Land, 10 returned saying: *"The people whom we saw in it are men of great size...and we became like grasshoppers in our own sight, and so we were in their sight"* (Numbers 13:32-33).

Only two spies, Joshua and Caleb, reported a land filled with milk and honey, exclaiming, *"We should by all means go up and take possession of it, for we will surely overcome it"* (Numbers 13:30). They believed God would deliver the land into their hands.

Ten of the spies brought a fear-filled report. In essence,

they said, "We saw giants in the land. There is no way we can take this country." Their fear and lack of faith struck terror into the hearts of the children of Israel.

Instead of remembering how God delivered them from the land of Egypt...

...the mighty miracles God performed with the plagues He brought against the Egyptians

...how God opened the Red Sea and swallowed Pharaoh and his army

...how God miraculously fed them in the wilderness for 40 years

...how the Almighty gave them water to drink

...how He supernaturally cared for them, not even allowing the sandals on their feet to wear out.

Instead of remembering these marvelous things, they chose to believe a negative report—to doubt God and His ability to drive out the inhabitants of the land He had told them to enter.

On the threshold of the Promised Land, all 12 of the spies saw the giants. But only 10 of them viewed themselves as grasshoppers, while the other two spies saw God!

Allowing fear to rule their hearts, the people chose to believe the grasshopper report. Is it any wonder that as the consequence of their faithlessness, God allowed the children of Israel to wander aimlessly in the wilderness for 40 years until the entire generation of grumbling, complaining, faithless people had died?

When you look at the circumstances you face and the choices you must make, are you like the 10 spies who were filled with fear and saw themselves as inferior "grasshoppers"? Or, are you like the two spies who saw God and had faith to believe that their victory was assured?

You have the right to choose to see the Lord—to

believe He will do what He says He will do—and to live by the promises of His Word!

REWARDS OF RIGHT CHOICES

Throughout the Bible, we're given examples of God's promised rewards or consequences:

- When you *choose* to allow other people to tell you something different from what God has told you, bad things happen (1 Kings 13).

- When you *choose* to put your faith in others instead of in God, He says your consequences are going to be His judgment (2 Kings 1).

- When you *choose* to be unfaithful to the Lord, He will *choose* to humble you (2 Chronicles 28). You may cry out, "Lord, I thought I lived under Your grace. I thought I was under the cloud of Your forgiveness. Why am I going through this?" And God responds, "You *chose* to be unfaithful to Me, despite what My Word says."

- When you *choose* to follow a plan that is not God's, He warns: "*Woe to those who choose to execute a plan that is not the Lord's, who choose to make an alliance that is not of His Spirit, who go to the world to take refuge and safety. Your reward will be shame and humiliation*" (2 Chronicles 28).

- When you *choose* to walk according to the stubbornness of your own heart and don't listen to the Lord, He will declare calamity against you (Jeremiah 16).

HOWEVER...

- When you *choose* to be persistent with God, He will hear and answer your prayers (2 Kings 4; Luke 18:1-8).

- When you *choose* to spend time in His presence, then His peace, blessings, and prosperity come (1 Chronicles 13).

Do you need peace today? Do you need blessings? Do you need prosperity? Spending time in His presence will provide you with all of these!

• When you *choose* to praise God and give Him thanks in the face of your adversity, you will be rewarded with victory (2 Chronicles 20). Are you facing a problem today? Do you need an answer to prayer? Praise and worship God, giving Him thanks for answering your prayer even before you see it come to pass, and see what God will do!

• When you *choose* to humble yourself before God, His Word says He will hear you (2 Chronicles 34). Choose today to humble yourself before Him!

• When you *choose* to return to the Lord, He says you will find compassion, mercy, grace, and forgiveness. Do you need these blessings from Him today? Then draw near to Him, and He will draw near to you (James 4:8).

I love the verse in John 15:16 where the Lord makes it clear that He made a choice. He *chose* you and ordained that you should go and bring forth fruit, and that your fruit should remain.

THE GREATEST CHOICE

In His divine plan to provide His children a way of escape from sin, Almighty God sent His only Son to earth—to be born as a man and to die on the Cross for our iniquity. Our salvation is a matter of choice—God's and ours.

Scripture records: *"God so loved the world, that he gave his only begotten Son* [God's choice] *that whosoever believeth in him* [our choice] *should not perish, but have everlasting life* [our reward]" (John 3:16 KJV).

I have met those who say, "It's wonderful that Jesus

came to earth so that I can live with Him forever in Heaven!" They believe their future is the result of God's decision, not theirs. But that's not how salvation works. Of course Jesus shed His precious Blood on the Cross for you and me, but we must—with an act of our will—choose to ask Him to forgive us.

Scripture proclaims: *"If you confess with your mouth Jesus as Lord, and believe in your heart that God raised Him from the dead, you will be saved; for with the heart a person believes, resulting in righteousness, and with the mouth he confesses, resulting in salvation"* (Romans 10:9-10).

The most important choice God will ever ask you to make is to accept or to reject the gift of His Son—Jesus Christ—and to make Him the Lord of your life. The consequence of that choice determines *where* you're going to spend eternity. But other choices you make in life, your attitude and actions, unlock the door to God's rewards and determine *how* you're going to spend eternity.

TOTAL FORGIVENESS

There are many who believe that they can never be forgiven and reconciled to God because they have made such horrendous mistakes and bad choices that their actions are unpardonable.

A man recently said to me, "You know, Dave, the things I have done in my life are so bad I don't see how God could ever forgive me. So why should I even try to live a Christian life?" I assured him the Lord *can*—He *will*—and He *does*—forgive us when we repent and ask for His forgiveness.

The Word declares: *"As far as the east is from the west, so far hath he removed our transgressions from us"* (Psalms 103:12 KJV). We also know, *"If we confess our sins, he is faithful and just to forgive us our sins, and to cleanse us from all unrighteousness"* (1 John 1:9 KJV).

The Lord can certainly redeem our wrong choices. However, just because the Lord wipes our slate clean and gives us a new beginning does not mean we avoid all the consequences of our past actions.

Let's be realistic. The wrong we have done may not only affect us—it may affect others as well. And even when we are redeemed by Jesus' blood, our wrong choices can still affect our health, our reputation, our finances, our relationships, and our right to be in leadership.

God absolutely will forgive our sins when we ask Him to. We have His Word on it! He is just and merciful. It's great to know that each and every morning, when we wake up and open our eyes, God renews His grace and mercy to us. I can tell you from personal experience, *"The Lord's loving kindnesses indeed never ceases, for His compassions never fail. They are new every morning; Great is Your faithfulness"* (Lamentations 3:22-23).

Regardless of your past, God's grace is sufficient. *If* we make the choice to turn from our sinful ways, humble ourselves, pray, seek His face and repent, we are sure to receive that grace. His faithfulness toward us is great!

A HEART-CHANGING EXPERIENCE

Have you ever personally asked Jesus Christ to be the Lord of your life? If not, would you consider making this life-changing choice today? If so, I'd love for you to pray these simple words with me:

Heavenly Father, I come before You now in the name of Your Son Jesus, asking You to forgive me for my sins. Jesus I ask You to come into my heart and be the Lord and Savior of my life. I believe You are the Son of God. I believe You died on the Cross and shed Your blood for my sins. I believe You rose from the grave, conquering death and hell for all eternity. Make me Your child right now. Wipe away my past and give me a whole new beginning. Lord, create in me a strong desire to study Your Word and spend time talking with You and worshiping You so I will grow and mature in my relationship with You. I ask and receive this in Your name, Lord Jesus. Amen!

Without question, asking Jesus Christ to forgive your sins, come into your heart, and become the Lord of your life is the most important decision you will ever make. It is a heart-changing experience that, with the guidance of the Holy Spirit, will help you make the best possible choices for the rest of your life.

4

BIG DOORS SWING ON SMALL HINGES

*Large streams from
little mountains flow;
tall oaks from little acorns grow.*

DAVID EVERETT

People thought Wilbur and Orville Wright were crazy! The two brothers from Ohio had traveled all the way to Kitty Hawk, North Carolina, to test a contraption they believed could rise above the earth and actually fly.

On a cold, windy morning in December 1903, after three days of failure, the Wright's "aeroplane" made it off the ground for 12 seconds—flying just 120 feet. They repeated their efforts throughout the day, finally hovering above the ground for 59 seconds and traveling 852 feet.

That doesn't sound like much of an achievement, yet for the first time man had defied the pull of gravity in a heavier-than-air craft. That small beginning transformed our world in ways no one could have imagined at the time.

Many years later, on July 20, 1969, Neil Armstrong stepped out of the Apollo spacecraft and placed his foot on the moon, saying, "That's one small step for man, one giant leap for mankind."

What a long journey from Kitty Hawk to the moon!

BEYOND IMAGINATION

Many of the dramatic turning points of civilization didn't seem exceptional at the time:

- Who could have dreamed of the great reformation that occurred in the church after Martin Luther nailed his *95 Theses* on the door of the Castle Church in 1517?

- On Christmas night, 1776, George Washington crossed the Delaware River and caught the British troops by surprise. It was a defining moment of the American Revolution that changed world history.

- In 1965, a computer in Massachusetts was connected

with one in California through a low-speed, dial-up telephone line. Today the world communicates at lightning speed via the Internet.

UNEXPECTED TURNING POINTS

When I talk with people about the memorable turning points of their lives, I am often amazed to hear how an insignificant event had major consequences. If you think for a moment, perhaps you can recall such an event in your life. Perhaps it was a casual conversation with someone that resulted in a new, exciting career, or an unexpected introduction that led to a permanent relationship.

This was certainly true for me. I was in a discount department store in Tulsa, Oklahoma, buying some materials to decorate my dorm room at Oral Roberts University when I struck up a conversation with the attractive checkout girl. You guessed it...she is now my wife, Barbara, and the mother of our children!

Never ignore or minimize the minor assignments of life. If your pastor or employer asks you to help with a task, however small, do it cheerfully as unto the Lord. After all, He is aware of every action of our daily life and every motivation of our hearts.

Jesus declares: *"He who is faithful in a very little thing is faithful also in much; and he who is unrighteous in a very little thing is unrighteous also in much"* (Luke 16:10).

Your "ministry" may include cleaning the church kitchen in preparation for a family night or changing diapers in the nursery during the service. Remember: God knows exactly where you are and what you are presenting to Him. He often places you in a "boot camp," making you ready for an important assignment of His choosing. Don't overlook or underestimate God's question: *"Who has despised the day of small things?"* (Zechariah 4:10)

SMALL BUT MIGHTY!

The most powerful forces are often controlled by tiny objects we may never see. For example, James tells us to *"Look at the ships...though they are so great and are driven by strong winds, are still directed by a very small rudder wherever the inclination of the pilot desires"* (James 3:4).

James was emphasizing an important Biblical principle. In the next verse, he continues: *"So also the tongue is a small part of the body, and yet it boasts of great things. See how great a forest is set aflame by such a small fire!"* (vs. 5-6)

So often, we desire the biggest, the greatest, and the highest. When the apostles learned the value of faith, they wanted more, asking Jesus: *"Increase our faith!"* (Luke 17:5) Listen to the Lord's reply: *"If you had faith like a mustard seed, you would say to this mulberry tree, 'Be uprooted and be planted in the sea'; and it would obey you"* (v. 6).

Never forget: when God is involved—and faith and obedience are added—a little is all that is needed.

The small village of Bethlehem may not have garnered much attention in its day, yet it would be where the greatest event of history would take place—where the Savior of the world would be born. Centuries before, God spoke through the prophet Micah, saying, *"As for you, Bethlehem...Too little to be among the clans of Judah, from you One will go forth for Me to be ruler in Israel. His goings forth are from long ago, from the days of eternity"* (Micah 5:2).

To God, Bethlehem was not an obscure place, but a *holy* city.

ONLY A "MITE"

One day Jesus was in the Temple at Jerusalem watching the rich place their gifts into the treasury. Then He saw something that instantly caught His attention: a poor widow putting in two small copper coins called "mites" worth about one-third of a cent each.

The Lord responded with praise: *"Truly I say to you, this poor widow put in more than all of them; for they all out of their surplus put into the offering; but she out of her poverty put in all that she had to live on"* (Luke 21:3-4).

To this woman, it didn't matter that she wasn't dressed in the fashion of the day or that the leading members of the community ignored her presence. She went to the Temple with one objective: to worship the Lord with her giving, knowing He is no respecter of persons. And so she gave all the money she had to God.

To me, the exceptional part of the story is the fact *Jesus was watching!* At the precise moment she gave her gift, I'm convinced the Lord began preparing a great reward for her.

THE MULTIPLICATION FACTOR

Many would maintain, "Since I have practically nothing to give, why should I give at all? What difference can it make?" My friend, the small thing God has placed in your hand is awesome when it is combined with the power of Almighty God!

• The widow at Shunem had nothing in her house but a jar of oil. Yet, because of her faith and obedience to the Prophet Elisha's words, God multiplied what she had given and worked a miracle of provision. Every available vessel was suddenly filled to the brim, and the Prophet said, *"Go, sell the oil and pay your debt, and you and your sons can live on the rest"* (2 Kings 4:7).

• Young David only had five smooth stones for his slingshot when he came against the mighty Goliath. But that's all the Lord needed. The Bible records that when David slung the first stone, it *"struck the Philistine...And the stone sank into his forehead, so that he fell on his face to the ground"* (1 Samuel 17:49). Many people pass over the point that David selected *five* smooth stones from the brook. However, this wasn't because he expected to miss the mark the first time. Did you know that Goliath had four brothers? He did! You can read the story in 2 Samuel 21. When David chose those five stones, it was as though he was saying, "Goliath this one is for you! And I've got four more for your brothers!" David trusted God's faithfulness to work through him and bring about the victory!

• When Jesus was speaking to a large crowd on the shore of Galilee and lunchtime approached, one of His disciples said, *"There is a lad here who has five barley loaves and two fish, but what are these for so many people?"* (John 6:9) From such meager resources, the Lord miraculously fed more than 5,000 people.

ONE TINY WORD!

As you study God's Word, you soon realize that your entire future hinges on one of the shortest words in the Bible: *"IF."*

Our Heavenly Father desires to enter into divine covenants with us and fulfill great promises to us, yet His covenants are *conditional.* Again and again, He announces that *if* we do our part—*then* He will do His part.

God told the people through His servant, Moses: *"Now*

it shall be, IF you diligently obey the Lord your God, being careful to do all His commandments which I command you today...All these blessings will come upon you and overtake you" (Deuteronomy 28:1-2).

Look at just a few of God's promises from Deuteronomy 28 that you can claim *IF* you choose to obey Him:

- The Lord will set you high above all the nations of the earth (v. 1).
- You will be blessed in the city and in the country (v. 3).
- Your offspring will be blessed (v. 4).
- Your herds will be increased (v. 4).
- *You will be blessed when you come in or go out.* (v. 6).
- Your enemies will flee (v. 7).
- The Lord will bless everything you put you hand to (v. 8).
- Your land will be blessed (v. 8).
- You will be established in God's holiness and image. (v. 9).
- You will abound in prosperity (v. 11).
- God will prosper you from "His good storehouse" and send rain to water your land. (v. 12).
- You will be a lender, not a borrower (v. 12).
- *God will make you "the head and not the tail," setting you above all of your circumstances* (v. 13).

This is the good news, isn't it? And all of these amazing blessings were prefaced by the tiny word "IF."

But there's another side to the "IF" message. Here are a few of God's promises from Deuteronomy 28 about what will happen *IF* you choose to *disobey* Him:

- You'll be cursed in the city and in the country. (v. 16).
- Your children will be cursed (v. 18).
- Your crops and herds will be cursed (v. 18).
- "Cursed shall you be when you come in, and cursed shall you be when you go out" (v. 19).
- You will have confusion and rebuke in everything you undertake (v. 20).
- You will have pestilence and ill health (vs. 21-22).
- You will experience a shortage of rain. (v. 24).
- You will be tormented by birds and wild animals. (v. 26).
- You will be oppressed and robbed continually, with no one to save you (v. 29).
- These curses shall affect you and your descendants forever. (v. 46).
- You will be under attack from enemies. (v. 49).
- You will be scattered throughout the earth (v. 64).

What a stark, contrasting set of consequences, all of which are the outcome of how you choose to respond to the word "IF"!

SMALL CHOICES, BIG RESULTS

Moses is another great example to us. The children of Israel needed water—after all, three million people in the hot desert required plenty to drink. God said to Moses, *"Speak to the rock"* (Numbers 20:8).

If you recall the story, you may remember that Moses struck the rock with his rod. Some people read the story and think Moses' disobedience was that he struck the rock twice instead of once. That's not correct. God had told Moses just to *speak* to the rock this time. But because Moses was angry with the people, he instead *chose* to disobey God's instructions, he and *struck* the rock.

What was the consequence of that seemingly small and insignificant choice of disobedience? Moses forfeited his role of leadership and lost his right to enter the Promised Land of milk and honey.

Oh, the consequences of that small act! God told Moses that Joshua would now lead the people into the Promised Land (Numbers 20:12, 27:15-23).

Friend, don't let what seems like a small or trivial choice can keep you from the destiny God has chosen for you!

THE DOMINO EFFECT

Perhaps you've known people who have allowed what may seem like a minor decision to develop into a fire raging out of control. Left unattended, just one character flaw can mushroom into a crisis.

And let's be clear about this: The Lord doesn't cause the problem—we do. James tells us what can happen when we choose to indulge in a temptation: *"Let no one say when he is tempted, 'I am being tempted by God; for God cannot be tempted by evil, and He Himself does not tempt anyone"* (James 1:13). The decision to sin is ours, and ours alone.

Even more dangerous, what begins as a trivial matter

can take on a domino effect, triggering consequences that grow progressively worse: *"Each one is tempted when he is carried away and enticed by his own lust. Then when lust has conceived, it gives birth to sin; and when sin is accomplished, it brings forth death"* (James 1:14-15).

Unless we repent, this destructive path leads from bad to worse: lust—sin—death. And it all begins when we choose to yield to temptation.

A TRIUMPHAL LIFE

Let's choose to travel a more satisfying route—one that leads from where we are to the place where God desires for us to be.

The Lord wants us to know that He has given us everything we need for a life of victory and fruitfulness. Peter writes:

> *His divine power has granted to us everything pertaining to life and godliness, through the true knowledge of Him who called us by His own glory and excellence. For by these He has granted to us His precious and magnificent promises, so that by them you may become partakers of the divine nature, having escaped the corruption that is in the world by lust* (2 Peter 1:3-4).

However, Peter also points out that we have a vital role to play in this life of victory:

> *Now for this very reason also, applying all diligence, in your faith supply moral excellence, and in your moral excellence, knowledge, and in your knowledge, self-control, and*

in your self-control, perseverance, and in your perseverance, godliness, and in your godliness, brotherly kindness, and in your brotherly kindness, love (2 Peter 1:5-7).

These spiritual attributes are not to remain stagnant, but are to multiply and expand: *"For if these qualities are yours and are increasing, they render you neither useless nor unfruitful in the true knowledge of our Lord Jesus Christ"* (v. 8).

When you reach your final destination, Jesus desires to say to you: *"I know your deeds, and your love and faith and service and perseverance, and that your deeds of late are greater than at first"* (Revelation 2:19).

So don't focus on your less-than-stellar beginnings. They are in the past. Start *"reaching forward to what lies ahead"* (Philippians 3:13).

The Lord stands waiting beside a door of great promise. He invites you to enter into a more intimate relationship with Him—and a life of greater joy than you've ever known before.

5

HOW CHOICES AFFECT YOUR PERSONAL LIFE

He who chooses the beginning
of a road chooses the place it leads to.
It is the means that determines the end.

HARRY EMERSON FOSDICK

Barbara and I have lost count of the number of women who have said to us, "I made a choice to marry a man. He loved me, but he didn't know the Lord. I knew the Bible told me not to be unequally yoked together with an unbeliever, but I loved him, and I thought it would all work out. I thought God would speak to his life through me, and I could change him."

Years later, she is crying, "Oh, Lord, if only I had listened to You. If only I had obeyed Your Word and not married an unbeliever!" Often their marriage ends in shambles with much pain and sadness.

How many people—and not just the young—in the height of some emotional moment choose to engage in sexual promiscuity? "Oh, one time won't hurt," they reason. But it *does* hurt. "No one will ever know." But somehow, they are found out. "God will forgive me." And He will. But what about the consequences?

In one moment, an unwanted pregnancy occurs and the "perfect" plan of God is thwarted. The consequences often include a ruined future, and the "wages" of their sinful decision will be paid for a lifetime.

Yes, God can forgive you. Yes, God can bring good out of a wrong choice. He can cover you with His mercy, grace, and forgiveness. But often the consequences aren't very easy to deal with.

It's so important for young and old alike to decide what standards they will set for themselves regarding dating, courtship, and marriage. They need to answer these questions early in the relationship:

- What are the boundaries we will not cross?
- Do we want our relationship to meet the standards of God's Word?

• Do we want our behavior to be pleasing in the Lord's sight? It is crucial to lay a strong, Biblical foundation right from the beginning of any relationship!

THE PRICE OF FRIENDSHIP

Parents plead with their teens, "Make the right choices in selecting your circle of friends"—yet kids often have difficulty understanding this warning. They don't realize the dangers lurking ahead.

We know a family whose son became friends with a group of young men who are on the wrong side of the law. These "friends" were involved in gangs, drugs and robbery.

"Oh, don't worry," the boy said, "I know where to draw the line. These guys are really fun to be around. Underneath, they're okay!" But the price of such friendships isn't worth the risk.

I had a chance to speak to this teen and seized the opportunity to warn him: "As long as you hang around with these individuals and make them your friends, you're playing with fire. Their environment and influence on you will be much stronger than you can imagine."

I could see the consequences ahead and cautioned him: "Before you know it, you'll be drawn into what they are doing because you'll want to be part of the group. The time will come when your continued association with them will be dependent on your doing certain things to prove your loyalty to them. There will come a day when you run out of options. Choosing to be part of a gang is not a halfway commitment. You're either 'in' or you're 'out.'"

Later, when the young man left, all I could do was pray for God's protection over him and ask God to somehow get a hold of him and turn his life around.

IS IT CONTAGIOUS?

You may not be faced with a situation as serious as the association of gang members, yet the people with whom you surround yourself and the friends you choose are critical to your success in life.

Do you choose to stay in the company of people who are negative, complaining, and constantly unhappy? Are these the individuals you allow to speak into your life?

This is a vital decision for you to make: You can decide to remain in such relationships, or you can back away, praying that God will help change their pessimistic outlooks.

The Bible speaks often concerning holiness—and *unholiness.* Unfortunately, many God-fearing people believe that holy living is contagious. It's not. They think, "If I live a righteous life before the world, unbelievers will be drawn to me and come to know the Lord."

Of course, in order to win people to Christ, you need to have communication with them, yet you should not make them your close buddies. Paul warned: *"Do not be bound together with unbelievers; for what partnership have righteousness and lawlessness, or what fellowship has light with darkness?"* (2 Corinthians 6:14)

According to the Bible, if you touch something spiritually unclean, *you* can become spiritually unclean. Your purity can be contaminated—not the other way around. As Job asked, *"Who can make the clean out of the unclean?"* (Job 14:4)

This same parallel of truth is found in the physical world. Take a look at something as simple as an infection. If you are exposed to a bacteria or disease, you can easily become infected and then transmit the bacteria to someone else.

I've heard the excuse, "I stay around this person because I'm hoping he will change." Wishing, hoping and even praying is fine, but don't allow your life to be tarnished by associating with others who clearly are living outside of God's will.

BARRIERS FOR OUR PROTECTION

God knew exactly what He was doing when He designed and created man:

- He made us with eyelids so we can shut out what we don't need to see.
- He designed our neck so we can turn away from evil.
- He fashioned our mouth so that we could close our lips and avoid speaking what is harmful to others.

Sadly, most people have not placed filters or erected barriers regarding what they choose concerning the television they watch, the movies they attend, the books and magazines they read, or the music lyrics they allow to enter their mind.

Perhaps you flip on the television and leave it on as background noise during your daily routine. Let me assure you that it is much more than "noise." Scripture tells us *"words...are spirit, and they are life"* (John 6:63). We also know that *"Death and life are in the power of the tongue"* (Proverbs 18:21).

Why does this matter? If you choose to watch an immoral television program, that same spirit permeates the air—and will invade *your* spirit.

You may be casually watching TV and say, "Oh, that sounds interesting." At first there may not be anything suggestive in the program—then, wham, there it is!

What do many of us do? We think, "This scene will be over in just a moment. Let's get past this garbage so I can see the end of the program." We tolerate the bad, hoping to return to the good.

Some even exclaim, "Oh, isn't that terrible! I can't believe what they're doing on TV!" Yet, they stay glued to the screen, complaining the entire time. It is far better to take the remote control in your hand and with one "click," say, "I'm not watching that!" Or, if you are reading a novel that is peppered with filthy language and trashy innuendos, close the book and throw it away!

THE INVASION

So many Christians wonder, "Why am I in a spiritual battle all the time?"—not realizing how the invasion has taken place. They have made a *choice*. Even without associating physically with ungodly people, they have allowed Satan to creep into their mind and spirit.

The moment we welcome wickedness—whether through a personal relationship or an inanimate object such as the internet or a TV program—we become friends with evil. King Jehoshaphat was asked, *"Should you help the wicked and love those who hate the Lord and so bring wrath on yourself from the Lord?"* (2 Chronicles 19:2). I believe you already know the answer. We need to follow the example of King David, who declared, *"I will set no wicked thing before mine eyes"* (Psalm 101:3).

The Lord does not turn a blind eye to the actions of His people. He is watching us as individuals and as a nation. When we abandon self-control and become more concerned with personal gratification than with glorifying God, there is trouble on the horizon. Scripture tells us: *"The Lord humbled Judah because of Ahaz king of Israel, for he had brought about a lack of restraint in Judah and was very unfaithful to the Lord"* (2 Chronicles 28:19).

Does this verse sound familiar? I think we can conclude that we are experiencing a lack of restraint across America and most other nations today.

DRAWING THE LINE

I'm sure you have heard the saying, "You are what you eat." Research tells us we also become what we watch and listen to. Our style, language, and behavior are often shaped by what we see and hear through the media.

It is vital that we make a conscious effort to filter out anything that does not uplift or build our inner person. We need to monitor both the quantity and the quality of the information entering our homes and our heart. The apostle Paul wrote, *"All things are lawful, but not all things are profitable. All things are lawful, but not all things edify"* (1 Corinthians 10:23).

God has given His people the discernment to know right from wrong. He expects us to take charge of the environment in our homes and lives. We must set guidelines regarding the...

...places we go.

...things we do.

...things we listen to.

...programs and movies we watch.

Dozens of times each day, we all make choices regarding what will or won't be a part of our lives. We must have the spiritual fortitude to maintain strong convictions, drawing a clear line of demarcation between good and evil.

DOES THE LORD APPROVE?

We've been talking about how decisions affect our personal relationships and the importance of staying pure before God. Yet this means grappling with choices at every stage of our growth and development. For example:

- Do I treat my body as the temple of the Holy Spirit?
- Do I care for my health, eating the right foods and exercising?
- What choices do I make to develop my gifts and talents?
- What decisions do I make to control my emotions?
- Are my choices promoting a Godly reputation?
- How do I avoid even the "appearance of evil" in my actions?
- What ethical choices am I making at work?

You may ask, "David, what is the most important thing I should consider when making personal decisions?" Let me answer by giving you an example from the Bible. King Jotham was only 25 years old when he began reigning over Jerusalem, and he ruled the city for 16 years. What was the secret of his success? The Bible records, *"Jotham became mighty because he ordered his ways before the Lord his God"* (2 Chronicles 27:6). He determined to model his life after the Almighty and was highly favored.

A few years ago, there was a national campaign to promote the acronym WWJD—What Would Jesus Do?

The letters adorned bracelets, T-shirts, bumper stickers, and posters. Here is a question we should continue to ask ourselves daily: **"Do my actions have God's divine stamp of approval?"**

6

HOW CHOICES AFFECT YOUR FAMILY

*A man ought to live so that
everybody knows he is a Christian—
and most of all, his family ought to know.*

DWIGHT L. MOODY

All people on earth have this in common: *We have all been children.* And we know firsthand how the decisions made by our parents have shaped and directed our lives.

Earlier I told you how I had to come to grips with the fact that my father was rarely home because of his call to international evangelism. Rather than becoming distraught and bitter, I chose to accept the call of God on Dad's life and on our family. Yet, deep in my heart I always thought, "When I grow up, it's going to be different. I'm not going to be away from my family."

Even though my focus was on the business side of the ministry, I found myself traveling more than I would have liked. Suddenly, I was faced with the same choice that my father had to make many years ago: Would I be willing to sacrifice time with my family to be in ministry? It wasn't an easy decision.

However, when Barbara and I decided to have children, I determined to be a stay-at-home dad as much as possible. I wanted to give my children the time and attention they deserved.

Did that decision mean I would have perfect teenagers who would never rebel and never cause us heartache or pain? Absolutely not. We were faced with the same challenges millions of parents experience. Nonetheless, this was a *choice* that I believed God was calling me to make for our family, and I have never regretted it.

As a father, I have learned that when I obey the Lord, He rewards both me AND my family with His blessings.

THE RIGHT DECISION

In 1990 Barbara and I uprooted our family and moved

from San Diego to Charlotte to lead The Inspiration Networks and Inspiration Ministries. Without question, it was a pressure-filled, traumatic time—especially for our children, who had to leave their friends behind. Yet Barbara and I prayerfully weighed the options and believed in our hearts we had made the right decision.

At that point in my life, God had given me many wonderful experiences—both in my spiritual life and in the corporate world. I had years of broadcast experience. I knew television production, understood media equipment, and knew how to design and build TV facilities.

Although there were plenty of miles on my life's speedometer, I was the first to admit I didn't know the world of cable television. As I told a friend, "I didn't know Cable from Mabel!"

Nevertheless, the decision had been made, and I totally immersed myself into the fascinating new arena of broadcasting. And what a baptism of fire it was!

THE VISION

It wasn't long before I began to hear God speaking to me about using the media as a tool to reach people for Christ. So much of Christian television was "by Christians, for Christians, and about Christianity," but where was the evangelism? What about the Lost? I began to see that most Bible-centered television had become a great "keeper of the aquarium" but not a very effective "fisher of men."

I saw how media—and television in particular—had taken center stage in our culture—probably becoming the most powerful force for change in the past 50 years. For better or for worse, television shapes and molds the minds and behavior of the billions of viewers who watch it.

Because of the decision we had made and our willingness to listen to the voice of the Master, He began giving me a vision. I started seeing television as a vital tool for discipleship and evangelism. I realized this tool could be used by God to impact the values, beliefs, behavior, attitude, and lifestyles of millions for His Kingdom—especially children and young people.

Praise God, it is happening! Since we launched these efforts in 1990, we have watched the Lord take this network from being available in barely three million homes to now being available in over 150 nations! Thousands of lives have been changed: families reunited, marriages restored, physical bodies healed, and Souls saved. We thank God for these victories.

The Lord also answered the cries of our hearts for our children, Ben and Becky. Today they both are married, raising their own families, and serving God.

These past years have not been without problems, but God has always been faithful. I've learned firsthand that He is a Rewarder of those who diligently seek Him (Hebrews 11:6). These blessings are the direct consequences of choices Barbara and I made.

"HERE AM I!"

Have you ever noticed how God's will seems to be progressive? When we answer, "Yes" to one assignment, He opens the next door to the next. Instead of revealing the whole picture all at once, He guides us one step at a time.

At one point, Barbara and I began to feel the Lord asking us to make another life-changing choice. God wanted to know, "Are you willing to step outside your comfort zone in the world of business and move into direct, personal ministry?"

Oh, if you only knew how much I chaffed at that thought! I became an ordained minister in 1974, but my "ministry" was business. The Lord had blessed me with abilities in that area, and I felt comfortable. Yes, my life involved God's work, yet always in a supportive role—rarely in a pulpit. I wrestled with God. "Why? Why me? Why now? Ask someone else."

Perhaps you remember the Bible story when God called Samuel. When the young boy heard the voice of the Lord, he answered, *"Here am I"* (1 Samuel 3:4).

Hard as it was at the time, this was also my response to God's call. I know I have made mistakes and failed my Heavenly Father many times, yet I know that I can honestly look Him in the face someday and say, "Lord, whenever I heard Your call, whenever You placed a choice before me, I answered 'Yes!' I have never knowingly disobeyed something I felt You specifically calling me to do."

Now I was saying again, "Here am I, Lord. I will answer Your call." The result of that decision was for Barbara and me to host a daily television program, program and many Campmeeting broadcasts over the years. Once more, the Lord rewarded our choice. We have received literally thousands of testimonies from people who contacted our ministry and asked us to agree with them in prayer.

I am sharing all of this with you to emphasize this point: I am convinced that because we have made *choices* to obey God through the years, He has *rewarded* us by pouring out His abundant blessings on us, our children, and the ministry to which we have been called.

WISE COUNSEL

I had two great examples growing up: my mother and father. The choices they made Sowed Seeds into my life and taught me how to make God-honoring choices.

By your example and the decisions you make, you are Sowing Seeds into your children that will produce a lifetime of rewards. We see that evidenced throughout the Scriptures.

King David is one of many such examples. He *chose* to Sow Seeds into his son Solomon (1 Chronicles 22:12). The Seed David had Sown into Solomon—the words that David had spoken to his son—caused Solomon to respond to God one day by saying, "Give me wisdom." He didn't come up with that response to God all on his own. Long before God ever said to Solomon, *"Ask what I shall give you"* (2 Chronicles 1:7), David had Sown Seeds of wisdom and truth into his son's heart and mind.

When Solomon answered: *"Give Your servant an understanding heart to judge Your people to discern between good and evil. For who is able to judge this great people of Yours?"* (v. 10), the Lord was pleased with Solomon's answer.

God told Solomon that because he had not requested riches, long life, or the defeat of his enemies, He would not only give him wisdom, but He would bless him with much more. God declared: *"I have also given you what you have not asked, both riches and honor, so that there will not be any among the kings like you all your days"* (vs. 11-12).

The Seeds that you *choose* to Sow into your children will bring a lifetime of rewards for them as well—either for good or bad. I can confidently tell you that the wise counsel of a Godly father pays great dividends!

ARE YOU AN EXAMPLE?

You can't just talk the talk with your children—you must walk the walk before them. For example, you can speak to your child about the dangers of drugs and immorality until you are blue in the face, yet if you are living in sin, your child is likely to follow your example, not your words.

Even more, your *hidden* iniquities—the sins you think no one knows about—will affect the lives of those you love for generations to come. You may find forgiveness, yet these transgressions still will impact your children.

That's not my opinion, but God's declaration. The Word clearly states: *"The Lord is slow to anger and abundant in loving kindness, forgiving iniquity and transgression; but He will by no means clear the guilty, visiting the iniquity of the fathers on the children to the third and the fourth generations"* (Numbers 14:18).

Today, ask God to help you live a blameless life before your family—setting a Godly example—and Sowing Seeds of wisdom and righteousness into their lives.

TESTING THE BOUNDARIES

You may ask, "How should I respond when I've done my best, yet my children still make harmful choices?"

Don't panic! Regardless of how much you try to perfectly raise your kids, they will test your boundaries and cause sleepless nights. But remember, they are your children—your flesh and blood. We can't just "disown" them because we disagree with the decisions they make! They are not the first to make mistakes and, sadly, they won't be the last. We *all* have made poor choices at times—

including great men of God like David and Peter.

The best advice you can give your children (and yourself!) is to encourage them to repent sincerely before God for their sins and start over again. Just because a person fails once doesn't mean they are doomed to repeat the pattern. Talk about it with them. Pray about it together. Encourage them to make better choices next time.

If people never failed, God would not have spent so much time teaching us about His grace and mercy. These free gifts from the Father are for imperfect people who make wrong decisions and need to be restored.

Solomon writes, *"A righteous man falls seven times, and rises again"* (Proverbs 24:16). And I love the encouraging words of David about God's ability to restore those who have make mistakes: *"The steps of a man are established by the Lord, and He delights in his way. When he falls, he will not be hurled headlong, because the Lord is the One who holds his hand"* (Psalm 37:23-24).

FIVE CHOICES FOR PARENTS

Here are five specific choices you can make to help build a strong foundation for your sons' and daughters' lives:

1. Choose to instill God's Word.

Some parents have the attitude, "My children will read the Bible when they're ready." That's not how the Lord intends for Scripture to be taught. It must start early— initiated by *you!* The Bible says: *"You shall teach them* [God's instructions] *diligently to your sons and shall talk of them when you sit in your house and when you walk by the way and when you lie down and when you rise up"* (Deuteronomy 6:7).

By Sowing the Word into your son or daughter, you are

preparing for an Eternal Harvest. As Paul wrote to Timothy: *"From childhood you have known the sacred writings which are able to give you the wisdom that leads to salvation through faith which is in Christ Jesus"* (2 Timothy 3:15). What a priceless gift from God!

2. Choose to teach your children to obey the Lord.

More than once, I've heard a mother warn her youngster, "You'd better obey me!" Yet it's much more effective to teach the child the necessity of obeying the principles God has written in His Word. Through Moses, God told His people to *"return to the Lord your God and obey Him with all your heart and soul according to all that I command you today, you and your sons"* (Deuteronomy 30:2). Teach your child that obedience to God brings great rewards!

3. Choose to discipline your children in love.

Many parents carry the admonition to "spare the rod and ruin the child" to an extreme. As a result, their kids are beat up rather than brought up! Listen to what the apostle Paul recommends: *"Fathers, do not provoke your children to anger, but bring them up in the discipline and instruction of the Lord"* (Ephesians 6:4).

At the same time, don't believe the self-proclaimed experts who tell you, "If you are too hard on your children, they will lose all respect for you." It's just the opposite. As Scripture declares: *"We had earthly fathers to discipline us, and we respected them; shall we not much rather be subject to the Father of spirits, and live?"* (Hebrews 12:9) Godly training and loving correction are the twin pillars of character.

4. Pass wisdom and knowledge on to those you love.

The Bible tells you to *"keep your soul diligently, so that you do not forget the things which your eyes have seen and they do not depart from your heart all the days of your life; but make them known to your sons and your grandsons"* (Deuteronomy 4:9). As a child of God, you have been given a great heritage. Pass it on!

5. Chose to give both instruction and direction.

Don't ignore the wisdom of Solomon. *"Train up a child in the way he should go; even when he is old he will not depart from it"* (Proverbs 22:6). And what does God expect from someone who would be a leader in the church? *"He must be one who manages his own household well, keeping his children under control with all dignity"* (1 Timothy 3:4). You only have one chance to raise a child. Make it count!

"LIKE A CHILD"

My heart is always touched when I read the story of how Jesus reached out to children. I can picture the scene of parents bringing their young sons and daughters to Him just so that He could touch them.

However, the disciples—perhaps trying to protect the Lord from the crowd—rebuked those who brought the children. When Jesus saw what the disciples were doing, *"He was indignant and said to them, 'Permit the children to come to Me; do not hinder them; for the kingdom of God belongs to such as these"* (Mark 10:14).

Then Jesus taught this spiritual application: *"Truly I say to you, whoever does not receive the kingdom of God like a child will not enter it at all"* (v. 15). Finally, the Lord took the children in His arms *"and began blessing them, laying His hands on them"* (v. 16).

I pray the choices you make today regarding your children will be pleasing to God and in His perfect will. To be a Christian means to be Christ-like. As you walk in obedience to the Word, you not only are becoming the person He has planned for you to be, but you are shaping and influencing the lives of your children.

As King David chose to Sow wise Seeds into the life of his son Solomon, choose to Sow wise Seeds into your children. May you be able to say, *"I have no greater joy than this, to hear of my children walking in the truth"* (3 John 1:4).

7

HOW CHOICES AFFECT YOUR FINANCES

God will not merely judge us
on the basis of what we gave,
but also on the basis of what we did
with what we kept for ourselves.

ERWIN W. LUTZER

I'm sure you've read the news accounts of people who lived a modest or even an austere life. Yet when they died, neighbors were shocked to learn they had accumulated great wealth—even millions of dollars. What was their secret? These individuals made some significant choices regarding their spending and saving habits.

The same principle applies to any enterprise we undertake. As author Peter Drucker observes, "Whenever you see a successful business, someone once made a courageous decision."

Take a moment to reflect on these very important questions:

- Do you choose to operate on a budget and live within your means, or do you choose to get into bondage with debt?

- Do you choose to make wise financial investments and plan for the future—higher education, home, retirement, even vacations?

- Do you choose to give God your first fruits—your tithes and offerings—or do you choose to rob God (Malachi 3)?

- Do you choose to teach your children the value of money and God's principles of faithfully tithing the first fruits of their income, giving offerings to the Lord, and supporting His work?

A PERPETUAL PROMISE

Seedtime and Harvest is a principle designed by God. This is *His* plan—not one devised by ordinary man. What God established is true! For me, for you, for everyone!

After the flood, God made a promise to Noah. He

declared, "*While the earth remains, **seedtime and harvest,** and cold and heat, and summer and winter, and day and night shall not cease*" (Genesis 8:22). This divine law is a perpetual promise.

Talk to any farmer, and he will tell you that if you want to reap a Harvest, you must first plant Seed. As long as he holds the Seed in his hand, he will never experience a Harvest greater than what he is holding. The same principle applies not only to the crops we plant in the field, but also to our finances and even our spiritual blessings.

Ask yourself, "If I'm clutching Seed in my hand, how can I ever expect to Reap a Harvest?" The answer is, you can't! You need to let the Seed go and let it grow.

WHAT WILL YOU REAP?

Through the prophet Haggai, the Lord asks, "*Is the seed still in the barn? Even including the vine, the fig tree, the pomegranate and the olive tree, it has not borne fruit*" (Haggai 2:19).

There is a spiritual precept in "letting go" of your Seed and Sowing it into Good Ground. Paul writes, "*Whatever a man sows, this he will also reap*" (Galatians 6:7). You can't Sow hatred and expect to Reap love. You can't Sow anger and bitterness and then wait for a Harvest of peace and contentment.

You determine the crop! *Whatever* you Sow you will Reap. Only when you release to Him what you are holding does God begin to move. What you have Sown He begins to multiply.

I know from experience that when I ask God for a bountiful Harvest, He requires more of me: more of my time, more of my family, more of *everything!*

77

But what if our Harvest seems to be delayed, or we don't Reap the kind of Harvest we are expecting? One reason can be found in the book of Haggai. God says that when you *choose* to look after your own things—after your own house and not after the things of God or His house—you'll Sow much but Harvest little.

- You'll eat, but not be satisfied.

- You'll put on clothing, but not be warm.

- You'll earn wages, but find out that you put them into a purse with holes.

- God may call for a drought on the labor of your hands.

The message is clear. When you choose to hold on to your Seed instead of Sowing it, you'll never bear fruit. You'll be rewarded with no Harvest.

SUPERNATURAL PROVISION

During planting in the springtime, a farmer faces the uncertainties of the elements. Will the weather be kind to his crops and produce a great Harvest, or will it destroy his efforts and result in ruin?

As Christians, we also wonder what each year will bring. What will happen with the economy, the stock market, the unemployment rate, competition in the marketplace, and the unexpected financial burdens we didn't foresee? We can never be certain of anything but God's faithfulness!

This is why we need the protective hand of our Heavenly Father and His favor over our lives. The Lord expects us to be obedient to His Scriptural principles as we tackle the tasks He has placed before us.

Think about it...Besides prayer and fasting, what else can you do that will bring God's supernatural provision and protection to you life? The answer is: Sowing the Seed God has placed into your hands. When you do, this simple act of faith becomes a covenant between you and God that will not be broken, because God is *always* true to His Word.

You may ask, "How much should I Sow?" Let's turn the question around: How great is your need? How much do you want the Lord to bless and prosper you in both spiritual and earthly matters? The apostle Paul declares: *"He who sows sparingly will also reap sparingly, and he who sows bountifully will also reap bountifully"* (2 Corinthians 9:6).

TAKE AN INVENTORY

What is a Seed? It is a tiny beginning with a huge future. A Seed is anything that can become *more*. This can include your time, your love, your talent, your patience, your money, your prayers. God has given you a *storehouse* of Seed, and you need to take inventory. Stop worrying about what you don't have and begin to see what you *do* have.

Just as tiny acorns become giant oak trees, what you already possess can become mighty. Recognize what God has stored inside you. Don't bury or hide it—use it!

If what you are Sowing is not producing the Harvest you desire, change the Seed you're Sowing. Invest your time in prayer. Ask the Holy Spirit to reveal what you have been given—supernaturally and naturally—and Sow it into God's Kingdom and the lives of others.

God's way of thinking is much different from ours.

People typically say, "If you need something, hold on to what you have, and try to get even more." In contrast, God maintains, "If you need something, give it away, and *I* will give you more!"

Let's look at how the Lord spells out His plan for provision: *"Give, and it will be given to you. They will pour into your lap a good measure—pressed down, shaken together, and running over. For by your standard of measure it will be measured to you in return"* (Luke 6:38).

If you need a friend, be a friend. If you need money, give money. If you need help, assist someone else. When you act according to this scriptural principle, the Lord pours blessings back into your life. Do you see why I prefer God's economy over the world's economy?

DON'T BE IN A HURRY!

Slow down! Be patient and wait long enough for your investment to produce the desired Harvest.

The Bible says, *"The Lord is good to those who wait for Him, to the person who seeks Him"* (Lamentations 3:25). Your waiting reveals trust: *"It is good that he waits silently for the salvation of the Lord"* (v. 26).

The delay may be painful at times, but there is a required season between Sowing and gathering the Harvest. Far too many people become discouraged and give up when they don't see immediate results.

Rarely are the results immediate when there is a process involved. Jesus says, *"The soil produces crops by itself; first the blade, then the head, then the mature grain in the head"* (Mark 4:28).

Give your Seed enough time to produce a Harvest. Harvests take time. No one plants rosebush seeds today and then expects to go out to the garden and pick roses tomorrow!

THE KEY TO PLENTY

Scripture is clear regarding supporting the work of the Lord with our giving.

When you choose to rob God of your tithes and offerings, the consequence is a curse. *"Will a man rob God? Yet you are robbing Me! But you say, 'How have we robbed You?' In tithes and offerings. You are cursed with a curse, for you are robbing Me, the whole nation of you!"* (Malachi 3:8-9)

But wait! By choosing to obey the Lord and Sowing your tithes and offerings into the storehouse of God, He will throw open the windows of Heaven and pour out blessings on you until they overflow (v. 10). Even more, the Lord will *"rebuke the devourer"* so that the fruits of your land will not be destroyed (v. 11).

When you make the decision to honor the Lord with your money—giving Him the first and best of what you have—you will always know plenty: *"Honor the Lord from your wealth and from the first of all your produce; so your barns will be filled with plenty and your vats will overflow with new wine"* (Proverbs 3:9-10).

But remember: Sowing is your choice; Reaping is God's reward!

WHAT IS GOD'S STOREHOUSE?

Many Christians today have difficulty understanding the concept of the storehouse of God. In the Old Testament, the storehouse was an actual storage room— a part of the Temple—where various things were stored for the service of the Temple. When something was needed by the priests for use in the Temple, they went to the storehouse and retrieved it.

The storehouse is God's place of *supply*. How does this apply to you today and where you should pay your tithes and offerings?

The answer is actually fairly simple: Where you are spiritually *supplied*, fed, and nourished. If this is your church—then your church is God's storehouse for you. If a particular radio or television ministry is a blessing to your spiritual life—then that is God's storehouse for you. If there is another ministry speaking into your life and bringing you spiritual supply—then that is God's storehouse for you.

If more than one place is spiritually *feeding* you, then each is entitled to a portion of your tithes according to the proportion of spiritual nourishment you are receiving from them. The reality is that most Christians today are spiritually fed and nourished from more than one storehouse. Each is deserving of a portion of their tithes.

Let me give you a parallel in the natural realm. If you go out to eat at a restaurant, where do you pay your bill? You pay your bill where you ate. You don't eat at one restaurant and then go across the street to another diner and pay your bill. That would be wrong. It's the same with your tithes.

HAVE FAITH IN GOD'S WORD!

It's not enough to simply read about the promises of God. It is critical that you have faith in God and activate His Word in your life.

One of the greatest examples of faith in the Bible is what took place in the life of Mary, the mother of Jesus. But where did Mary receive the faith to believe she would bear a child and that He would be the Son of God? This was unexpected news to her!

God was not relying on Mary's faith to work the miracle—just as the Lord is not restricted by your level of faith to bring forth what is needed in *your* life. What God was depending on with Mary—and what He is counting on in your circumstances—is the power of His Word! The Lord desires that we rely on and place our total trust in Scripture; not depending on ourselves, or our level of faith, but rather only on His Word.

When the angel told Mary she was going to bring forth a Son, she did not doubt or hesitate; she simply accepted the news and agreed, *"May it be done to me according to your word"* (Luke 1:38). The angel came with a message from God, yet Mary had to receive it by faith. In effect, she responded, "I believe what you have said. Let God's Word be true for me, even as you have spoken it!" This is the kind of expectant response God desires from us as well.

FIVE DIVINE PRINCIPLES

If your life is consumed by chasing material possessions and building your financial portfolio, stop for a moment to listen to these words of Jesus: *"What will it profit a man if he gains the whole world and forfeits his soul? Or what will a man give in exchange for his soul?"* (Matthew 16:26) Instead of living according to the world's economic plan, start obeying these divine principles:

1. Giving to God must come first.

"Honor the Lord from your wealth and from the first of all your produce; so your barns will be filled with plenty and your vats will overflow with new wine" (Proverbs 3:9-10).

2. When you choose to seek the Lord, God will abundantly bless you.

The Bible says concerning King Uzziah: *"As long as he sought the Lord, God prospered him"* (2 Chronicles 26:5). And Jesus declares: *"Seek first His kingdom and His righteousness, and all these things will be added to you"* (Matthew 6:33). Instead of asking yourself, "What am I Reaping?" ask, "What am I seeking?"

3. Don't give the Lord your leftovers.

According to His Word, when you choose to give the Lord your second best... your leftovers...the things that aren't important to you...He is not pleased, and He will not accept your offering (Malachi 1:6-10). According to Scripture, we are commanded to bring to the Lord the *first* of what we receive.

4. Give with a clean, forgiving heart.

Jesus teaches that when we choose to bring an offering to the Lord when we are at war with our brother, God will refuse our gift. He declares, *"First be reconciled to your brother, and then come and present your offering"* (Matthew 5:24). The Master also tells us that if we decide to practice our righteousness to be noticed and applauded by people, we will have no reward with our Father in Heaven (Matthew 6:1).

5. **Every act of kindness is an investment in eternity.**

When we decide to live for others rather than ourselves, we Reap great dividends. As Paul writes: *"Knowing that whatever good thing each one does, this he will receive back from the Lord"* (Ephesians 6:8). Your choice to make an investment in the lives of others is a treasure more valuable than silver or gold.

"ENLARGE MY BORDER"

We can *position* ourselves to receive God's favor. There is a verse in the Old Testament many of us had overlooked until Bruce Wilkinson called attention to it in his wonderful book, *The Prayer of Jabez.*

The Bible records that Jabez *"called on the God of Israel, saying, 'Oh that You would bless me indeed and enlarge my border, and that Your hand might be with me, and that You would keep me from harm that it may not pain me!' And God granted him what he requested"* (1 Chronicles 4:10).

Read this prayer again, and you will see that there are four vital parts to Jabez' request:

First: Jabez asks God to bless him.

Second: He asks the Lord to enlarge his territory, giving him more responsibility.

Third: He prays for God to stay close to Him.

Fourth: Jabez requests the Lord to protect him from pain and harm.

This is a prayer you can offer to God each day. When you do, you are asking your Heavenly Father to be at the center of every activity of your life, and you are affirming that your total reliance is on Him.

Now for the best part! God not only received the prayer of Jabez, but He *rewarded* him by granting his request! The

Word declares: *"The prayer of the upright is His delight"* (Proverbs 15:8).

The Lord will bring choices and opportunities into your life. They may not always be easy, but I promise that if you will make the decisions God desires, you will experience an abundant life, filled with His rewards— now AND in the life to come!

8

HOW CHOICES AFFECT YOUR SPIRITUAL LIFE

*The spiritually minded believer
makes his decisions on the basis of
eternal values and not on
the passing fads of society.*

WARREN W. WIERSBE

Have you ever been around people who are slaves to their schedule? Every minute of the week is accounted for, and they won't let *anything* interrupt their routine. Every moment is all written down—when they eat, sleep, work, exercise, watch their kids play soccer, go to a movie, turn on the television set, or visit Grandma. And, if God is fortunate enough, they might even set aside time for church on Sunday morning. One man, showing me the calendar on his new smart phone, told me, "I just don't know how I existed before I bought this thing!"

Many have *compartmentalized* their lives to such an extent that there is absolutely no time left for prayer, reading the Word, or building a foundation of faith. It is time for us all to pause and take a fresh, introspective look at our priorities. Every day we make choices that affect our family, our social life, and our finances, but what about our *spiritual life*? What are we doing that will bring a "God consciousness" to every event we undertake?

Rather than giving the Lord a few scattered minutes here and there, we need Him to be at the *center* of our thoughts and continually reflected in our actions. Instead, we say, "I'm going to pray the first thing every morning." However, God amazingly tells us: *"Pray without ceasing"* (1 Thessalonians 5:17).

We say, "I need to concentrate on making a living." However, Jesus says: *"Seek first His kingdom and His righteousness, and all these things will be added to you"* (Matthew 6:33).

The Spirit-led life comes from giving the Lord *everything*—your time, your talent, your today, and your tomorrow. Our spiritual lives must be more than a part-time trivial pursuit!

START EARLY

You are a new creation in Christ—and now it's time to grow spiritually.

Let's look at the life of Jesus when He was on earth. Yes, He was the Son of God, yet He still had a desire to learn and gain wisdom. When He was only 12 years old, Jesus traveled with His family and a group of people from Nazareth to Jerusalem for the Feast of the Passover. On the way home after the event, Mary and Joseph realized that Jesus wasn't with them. Three days later, they found Him in the Temple courts *"sitting in the midst of the teachers, both listening to them and asking them questions"* (Luke 2:46).

When they found Him, Mary exclaimed, *"Son, why have You treated us this way? Behold, Your father and I have been anxiously looking for You"* (v. 48).

Young Jesus replied, *"Why is it that you were looking for Me? Did you not know that I had to be in My Father's house?"* (v. 49) From that time forward, *"Jesus kept increasing in wisdom and stature, and in favor with God and men"* (v. 53).

Jesus made a *choice* to learn everything possible about the things of God.

OH, THE POTENTIAL!

Let's contrast this with another Nazirite who was born with an awesome potential for greatness. His name was Samson.

Even before he was born, an angel appeared and told his mother—who was barren and childless—that she would have a son set apart at birth: *"and he shall begin to deliver Israel from the hands of the Philistines"* (Judges 13:5).

89

We read how *"the child grew up and the Lord blessed him. And the Spirit of the Lord began to stir him"* (vs. 24-25).

Samson was chosen by God to be a ruler and judge over the children of Israel. The Lord had a plan for his life—one of leadership, responsibility, and position. He became a man of power, both in physical strength and national authority, who led Israel for 20 years. And what a reputation he enjoyed! Samson could tear lions apart with his bare hands (Judges 14:6) and defeat 1,000 men with the jawbone of a donkey (Judges 15:15).

Sadly however, Samson made some tragic choices that ruined him spiritually. He fell in love with a woman named Delilah, who then was offered money to discover and reveal the source of Samson's strength. He gave into the lust of the flesh, and, in a moment of weakness, told her everything, including this secret: *"A razor has never come on my head, for I have been a Nazirite to God from my mother's womb. If I am shaved, then my strength will leave me and I will become weak and be like any other man"* (Judges 16:17).

As Samson lay sleeping, Delilah shaved his head and alerted the Philistines. They rushed in, bound the shaven and weakened man with ropes, brought him to Geza where they gouged out his eyes, and forced him to grind grain in the prison house.

God had a glorious future designed for Samson, yet he threw it all away by making wrong decisions. His life ended when, with one final burst of his former power, he pulled down the pillars that supported a pagan temple crowded with Philistines. It must have been quite a scene. Scripture records: *"The dead whom he killed at his death were more than those whom he killed in his life"* (Judges 16:30).

Choosing sin and disobedience will blind and deceive

you, taking you hostage and finally destroying your life. Oh, what a difference when we listen to the voice of the Lord and obey His commands. It is the Father who *satisfies your years with good things, so that your youth is renewed like the eagle*" (Psalm 103:5).

SEEDS OF GROWTH

There is a direct connection between your choices and your spiritual growth—a clear "cause and effect" relationship. Here are a few examples:

1. By choosing to receive God's ultimate gift, you will grow in love.

It's almost impossible to fathom how much the Father cares for us. He demonstrated it when He sent His Son to earth. His Word tells us: *"In this is love, not that we loved God, but that He loved us and sent His Son to be the propitiation for our sins"* (1 John 4:10).

When we receive Christ, we receive the gift of His love so that we can share it with those around us: *"Beloved, if God so loved us, we also ought to love one another"* (1 John 4:11). As a result, the treasure God has placed within us multiplies.

2. By choosing to ask the Lord, you will grow in His wisdom.

The first step to *receiving* is *requesting!* As amazing as it may seem, the storehouse of an all-wise God is yours for the asking. James writes: *"If any of you lacks wisdom, let him ask of God, who gives to all generously and without reproach, and it will be given to him"*

(James 1:5). I encourage you to make this request: "Lord, You are the source of all knowledge and understanding, and I am asking for Your wisdom today."

3. **By choosing to draw near to God, you will grow in grace and mercy.**

There are no barriers to prevent us from approaching the Lord. His arms are outstretched. *"Therefore let us draw near with confidence to the throne of grace, so that we may receive mercy and find grace to help in time of need"* (Hebrews 4:16). *Whosoever* will may come!

4. **By choosing God's road, you will grow in joy.**

Your spiritual life is not meant to be one of drudgery or a daily grind. Rather, God's plan is for it to be just the opposite. The psalmist declares: *"You will make known to me the path of life; in Your presence is fullness of joy; in Your right hand there are pleasures forever"* (Psalm 16:11). That's why Paul tells us to rejoice in the Lord ALWAYS! (Philippians 4:4).

5. **By choosing righteousness, you will grow in courage.**

We were not born to cower in fear and retreat because of worry and anxiety. These are responses learned from living in a world of sin. God has a better plan: *"In right-eousness you will be established; You will be far from oppression, for you will not fear; And from terror, for it will not come near you"* (Isaiah 54:14). Ask the Lord to clothe you in His truth and set your feet on the Solid Rock so that you can combat every anxiety and live in triumph.

6. By choosing to receive the Lord, you will grow in hope and expectation.

Redemption is not only to free us from sin, but also to release us from negative thinking. As Paul declares: *"Christ in you, the hope of glory"* (Colossians 1:27).

Your source of optimism is not man-made—your source is *GOD!* Pray with the psalmist: *"My soul, wait in silence for God only, For my hope is from Him"* (Psalm 62:5). Remember: You are a child of promise —and that means you have a glorious future!

7. By choosing to act upon belief and trust, you will grow in faith.

Each of us has been given a *"measure of faith"* (Romans 12:3), yet this doesn't mean our faith can't increase. The apostles said to the Lord: *"Increase our faith!"* (Luke 17:5)—which means faith can grow and develop!

Faith is the essential ingredient for a victorious Spirit-filled life. We must live by it (Romans 1:17), walk by it (2 Corinthians 5:7, Romans 4:12), and use it to overcome the world (1 John 5:4, Ephesians 6:16).

DON'T LOOK BACK!

When you read the accounts of great battles—from Biblical times to modern warfare—you know that victory doesn't come when you decide to retreat. It's imperative to stay on the *offensive*. The same is true in our walk with the Lord. If we lay down our armor and stop moving forward, the opposite of spiritual growth occurs—we become discouraged, even powerless.

Don't ignore what God declares through the prophet Isaiah, who says *"woe"* to those *"who execute a plan, but not Mine, and make an alliance, but not of My Spirit"* (Isaiah 30:1). God warns those who run to the world to seek refuge and safety that they will Reap *"humiliation"* (v. 3).

Spiritual decline is a direct result of our stubborn, self-centered choices. The Lord says: *"Because I called and you refused, I stretched out my hand and no one paid attention; And you neglected all my counsel and did not want my reproof; I will also laugh at your calamity; I will mock when your dread comes"* (Proverbs 1:24-26).

"Refusing" and "neglecting" are choices we make. Why blame God for the consequences when we have been given every opportunity to make life-changing decisions?

YOUR PRIORITY

My friend, if you're looking for a sure-fire path to spiritual growth, spend time every day in God's presence. When you choose to make Him your top priority, you will know His peace, His blessing, and His provision!

In the Old Testament, the presence of the Lord was represented by the Ark of the Covenant. In one instance, during King David's reign, *"the ark of God remained with the family of Obed-edom in his house three months; and the Lord blessed the family...and all that he had"* (1 Chronicles 13:14).

Today, we don't have the physical Ark to which we can draw near and receive God's blessings. Yet something far better has occurred to bring us into the very Presence of the Lord. You see, when Christ died on the Cross, *"the veil of the temple was torn in two from top to bottom"* (Matthew 27:51). Now we can come *"boldly unto the throne of grace, that we may obtain mercy, and find grace to help in time of need"* (Hebrews 4:16 KJV).

Believe it or not, friend, when you choose to spend time in the presence of the Lord, one of the great consequences will be His blessing on your life. What God did for the household of Obed-edom, He will do for you! His presence brings blessings, and He is worthy of our praise and worship.

During one of the great battles in Israel, King Jehoshaphat and the army of Israel were so outnumbered by the enemy they didn't stand a chance (2 Chronicles 20:2).

What could Jehoshaphat do? God told him to appoint singers to go out ahead of the army to praise the Lord. The Bible records the miraculous result: *"When they began singing and praising, the Lord set ambushes against [those] who had come against Judah; so they were routed"* (v. 22). What a lesson! When you choose to praise and worship God in the face of your adversity, victory comes.

Lifting our voices to the Lord should not be limited to a Sunday church service. We need to *continually* spend time in His presence. When you face an impossibility, and don't feel you stand a chance, start giving the Lord honor and praise. Worship Him. You'll be surprised what the Lord will do for you!

OUR DAILY BREAD

In the wilderness, God miraculously provided manna for the children of Israel to eat, but they were only to collect enough food for one day at a time. What was collected one morning became rotten the next with a stench so bad that it made the people sick. Only on the sixth day was there manna that lasted *two* days—because God wanted them to keep the Sabbath holy (Exodus 16:5).

Part of what God was trying to teach the children of Israel through the manna experience was to be dependent on Him *every day*. He also wants *us* to know that we can't live today on yesterday's provision, yesterday's word, yesterday's experience. We need fresh manna and a fresh experience with Him every day! That's why Jesus said, *"Give us this day our **daily** bread"* (Matthew 6:11).

Regretfully, many Christians don't choose to spend time with the Lord daily—in His presence, in His Word, in prayer, and in worship. How can we expect to be fed and nourished by Him if we don't spend time with Him?

This is why—whether you realize it or not—you may be starving to death spiritually. Perhaps your spiritual life is malnourished and lacking the power you need to live an overcoming life. Yet this changes when you choose to faithfully spend time with the Lord every day!

STRENGTH FROM ABOVE

Spiritual growth is the result of *abiding* and *dwelling* with the Lord. That's a promise from God's Word: *"He who dwells in the shelter of the Most High will abide in the shadow of the Almighty. I will say to the Lord, 'My refuge and my fortress, My God, in whom I trust!'"* (Psalm 91:1-2).

What can you expect when you make the choice to trust completely in the Lord alone? He will...

...deliver you from Satan's snares (v. 3).
...become your Refuge and Protection (v. 4).
...remove the fear of terror (v. 5).
...shield you from harm (v. 6).
...send His angels to guard you (v. 11).
...honor you (v. 15).
...reward you with a long, satisfying life (v. 16).

And that's just the *beginning* of what the Lord will do for you!

Spending time reading God's Word daily is a form of spiritual exercise. We are *built up*—both in faith and in the knowledge of the Father—to the point that we become living examples of His strength and power.

This is what empowered the prophet Elijah and gave him such confidence in his showdown with hundreds of prophets of Baal on Mount Carmel. Elijah gave them an ultimate choice: *"How long will you hesitate between two opinions? If the Lord is God, follow Him; but if Baal, follow him"* (1 Kings 18:21).

Here was only *one* man of God coming against hundreds of zealous unbelievers, and complete belief in the Almighty was required to even issue such a challenge! Elijah announced:

> *Now let them give us two oxen; and let them choose one ox for themselves and cut it up, and place it on the wood, but put no fire under it; and I will prepare the other ox and lay it on the wood, and I will not put a fire under it. Then you call on the name of your god, and I will call on the name of the Lord, and the God who answers by fire, He is God* (vs. 23-24).

The people agreed to this plan.

The prophets of Baal tried first, but after pleading with their god from morning until noon, nothing happened. Elijah even taunted them, saying, *"Call out with a loud voice, for he is a god; either he is occupied or gone aside, or is on a journey, or perhaps he is asleep and needs to be awakened"* (v. 27). So Baal's prophets shouted louder, even slashing themselves with swords and spears until their blood flowed. And still there was no fire.

"AT YOUR WORD"

That same evening, Elijah repaired the altar. He took 12 stones—one for each tribe of Israel—and dug a trench around it. Then, after the wood and meat were in place, he asked that water be poured over the sacrifice, not just once, but *three times!* (v. 34).

The challenge had been made, and now it was God's turn. At that moment, Elijah looked up to heaven and spoke one of the most powerful prayers recorded in Scripture:

> *O Lord, the God of Abraham, Isaac and Israel, today let it be known that You are God in Israel and that I am Your servant and I have done all these things at Your word. Answer me, O Lord, answer me, that this people may know that You, O Lord, are God, and that You have turned their heart back again* (vs. 36-37).

What happened next? God's fire fell and burned up the sacrifice, the wood, the stones, the soil, and even the water in the trench. When the people saw this, they fell on their faces and cried, *"The Lord, He is God; the Lord, He is God"* (v. 39).

My friend, are you hesitating today in your choice to serve God? Are you hesitating to embrace His plans and purposes for your life? Hebrews 3:15 says, *"Today if you Hear his voice, and do not harden not your hearts, as when they provoked Me."* The choice is yours. The right choice will bring a lifetime of rewards, in this life AND in the life to come.

THE STARTING POINT

You may ask, "Where do I begin? How do I embark on the path to spiritual growth that God has planned for me?" Start with the nourishment of the Word. Listen to what Peter says about this: *"Like newborn babies, long for the pure milk of the word, so that by it you may grow in respect to salvation"* (1 Peter 2:2). Read God's Word, study it, and make it a disciplined part of your daily schedule, and your spiritual life will grow and become strong.

Next, develop a strong prayer life, getting to know your Heavenly Father through daily communion. Then, find a body of Believers with whom you can fellowship and sit under Spirit-filled teaching. When you add praise, worship, spiritual accountability, and righteous living, there's no cap or limitation to what the Lord will do in your life!

But it all starts with *your* choice.

HOW YOUR DECISIONS CAN DEFEAT THE DEVIL

*When you close your eyes
to the devil, be sure
it is not a wink.*

JOHN C. KULP

Everybody makes mistakes, but only some take responsibility for their actions: "What was I thinking? How could I have done such a stupid thing?"

From my observations, however, most people look for an excuse to blame anyone or anything other than themselves:

- A man pulled over for exceeding the speed limit asks the patrolman: "Where was the sign? I didn't see one posted!"

- A salesman caught padding his expense account says, "I was just trying to cover what it *really* cost me to make the trip."

- A student accused of plagiarizing part of a term paper, protests, "Was I supposed to write every word myself? I thought you wanted me to do some research!"

Eve was the first person to offer the excuse repeated by millions to this day: "The devil made me do it!" Is this true? Does Satan really exert that kind of power over you? Are your attitudes and actions really controlled by him? If so, what steps can you take to defeat this evil foe?

THE DECEIVER

Let's not fool ourselves—there is a real devil roaming the earth who is very much alive. *"Be of sober spirit, be on the alert. Your adversary, the devil, prowls around like a roaring lion, seeking someone to devour"* (1 Peter 5:8).

Satan is called the *"adversary"*—and he certainly is, to both God and man. He brings sin, disease, fear, torment and death. The devil is also a deceiver. Jesus declared: *"He was a murderer from the beginning, and does not stand in the truth because there is no truth in him. Whenever he speaks a lie, he speaks from his own nature, for he is a liar and the father of lies"* (John 8:44).

How do we know that Satan is the author of sickness? Because Jesus *"went about doing good and healing all who were oppressed by the devil"* (Acts 10:38). He also delivered a woman *"whom Satan has bound for eighteen long years"* (Luke 13:16).

Let there be no doubt: It is the devil who attacks our bodies, our souls, and our minds.

SATAN'S SCHEMES

As much as some people would like to ignore this subject, the reality is that Satan still prowls the land seeking to establish his devious plans. Paul tells us to stay alert, *"Lest Satan should take advantage of us; for we are not ignorant of his devices"* (2 Corinthians 2:11).

The devil delights in distracting our attention from the Lord. That's why we are warned: *"Do not love the world nor the things in the world. If anyone loves the world, the love of the Father is not in him"* (1 John 2:15).

Satan also tries to fill our mind with confusion and uncertainty. Jesus asks, *"Why are you troubled, and why do doubts arise in your hearts?"* (Luke 24:38) Do you remember when Peter walked on the water and then began to sink? The Master immediately stretched out His hand to take hold of him, asking, *"You of little faith, why did you doubt?"* (Matthew 14:31)

Satan tries to delay your spiritual progress. When Paul was to present his defense of the Gospel to Felix, the governor became frightened and said, *"Go away for the present, and when I find time I will summon you"* (Acts 24:25).

In the words of a German proverb, "When God says today, the devil says tomorrow."

DANGER AHEAD!

The highway patrol has a slogan to warn people what will happen to their license if they are caught driving while intoxicated: "Booze it and lose it!"

According to the Word of God, we can say much the same thing about sin: "Choose it and lose it!" When we select evil over righteousness, we are the losers—our prayers are not answered, and we are left without hope unless and until we repent before God. The people of Israel were *"defeated before an enemy, because they have sinned against You"* (1 Kings 8:33).

Let me remind you again that we are accountable for our choices, whether they be virtues or vices. The Lord will *"reward the doer of evil according to his wickedness"* (2 Samuel 3:39).

Now hear the *good* news! Jesus was sent to earth to foil and ruin the schemes and snares of Satan. According to the Word: *"The Son of God appeared for this purpose, to destroy the works of the devil"* (1 John 3:8).

Even more, Christ came to confront Satan himself. Jesus was crucified, *"that through death He might render powerless him who had the power of death, that is, the devil"* (Hebrews 2:14). My friend, I want you to know that Jesus Christ's victory at Calvary makes it possible for every Believer to take authority over Satan.

PLACE SATAN ON NOTICE

If we give the devil one minute of our attention, that's 60 seconds too much. Instead, start treating him as the defeated foe he actually is. Listen to the words of Jesus: *"Behold, I have given you authority...over all the power of the enemy"* (Luke 10:19).

According to Scripture, you can put Satan on notice that you are exempt from his evil attacks *"because greater is He who is in you than he who is in the world"* (1 John 4:4).

The next time the devil comes your way, don't flinch. You have been granted power from Heaven that will cause him to turn and run. How is that possible? *"Submit therefore to God. Resist the devil and he will flee from you"* (James 4:7).

The demons of hell are fearful of Jesus and depart when He commands them to leave. In one encounter, the demons cried to the Lord: *"What business do we have with each other, Jesus of Nazareth? Have You come to destroy us? I know who You are—the Holy One of God!"* (Mark 1:24). And then the demons fled!

The Holy Spirit will erect a barrier to stop Satan in his tracks. He won't be able to go any further. *"When the enemy shall come in like a flood, the Spirit of the Lord shall lift up a standard against him"* (Isaiah 59:19 KJV).

WE HAVE THE POWER!

It isn't only Jesus who is able to cast out demons. Look at what happened to a Believer named Phillip who traveled to Samaria to preach the Gospel of Christ. Reporting on that great revival, the Bible says, *"In the case of many who had unclean spirits, they were coming out of them shouting with a loud voice; and many who had been para-lyzed and lame were healed"* (Acts 8:7).

The apostle Paul also took authority over the enemy. A woman *"possessed with a spirit"* taunted the missionary evangelist in one city. After several days of her harass-ment, Paul was so annoyed that he turned and said to the spirit in her: *"'I command you in the name of Jesus Christ to come out of her!' And it came out at that very moment"* (Acts 16:18).

God was performing *"extraordinary miracles by the hands of Paul so that handkerchiefs or aprons were even carried from his body to the sick, and the diseases left them and the evil spirits went out"* (Acts 19:11-12).

It should come as no surprise that the followers of Jesus— including you and me –have the divine power He possesses. Before His ascension into Heaven, the Master announced: *"These signs will accompany those who have believed: in My name they will cast out demons, they will speak with new tongues; they will pick up serpents, and if they drink any deadly poison, it will not hurt them; they will lay hands on the sick, and they will recover"* (Mark 16:17-18).

From my experience in ministry around the world, I can tell you that miracles are occurring as never before— just as the Lord declared. He said: *"Truly, truly, I say to you, he who believes in Me, the works that I do, he will do also; and greater works than these he will do; because I go to the Father"* (John 14:12).

STAND IN YOUR AUTHORITY!

We have been given the same power today that is in the earthly ministry of the Lord Jesus. The Word con-firms: *"as He is, so also are we in this world"* (1 John 4:17).

So go ahead and boldly declare, "**I can take authority over Satan!**" Why? Because:

- "God says I can."
- "I am covered with the blood of Jesus Christ."
- "I am filled with His Spirit."
- "God's Word is in my heart."
- "God sends angels to protect me."
- "I speak in the name of Jesus."

Why allow the devil to pester you any longer? If Jesus can cause him to flee, so can you!

SIX DECISIONS

Don't buy into the notion that you can get rid of Satan by ignoring him. It doesn't work! Instead, defeat him by making these six decisions:

1. Decide to confront the devil with God's Word (Matthew 4:1-11).

2. Decide to deny Satan any opportunity (Ephesians 4:27).

3. Decide to resist the devil (Ephesians 6:13).

4. Decide to flee from temptation (Luke 22:40).

5. Decide to stay out of Satan's territory (2 Samuel 11:1-5).

6. Decide to take authority over evil (Jude 1:9). What Jesus said to Peter, He is also telling you: *"Whatever you bind on earth shall have been bound in heaven, and whatever you loose on earth shall have been loosed in heaven"* (Matthew 16:19).

With Satan on the attack, we can't afford to sit idly by. Confront him, bind him, and cast him out!

AN EXTRAORDINARY BATTLE

By God's grace and the prayers and support of our faithful Inspiration Partners, Inspiration Ministries is touching countless lives—both in the United States and in foreign nations. But I can tell you that Satan clashes with us over every cable household we attempt to enter and over every man, woman, boy or girl we reach with the Gospel.

You see, the battle in which we are engaged is not of this world. As Paul states:

> *The weapons of our warfare are not carnal, but mighty through God to the pulling down of strongholds; Casting down imaginations, and every high thing that exalteth itself against the knowledge of God, and bringing into captivity every thought to the obedience of Christ* (1 Corinthians 10:4).

The only way for us to triumph in this conflict against the enemy is to put on the whole armor of God, *"so that you will be able to stand firm against the schemes of the devil"* (Ephesians 6:11). Our struggle is not against flesh and blood, *"but against the rulers, against the powers, against the world forces of this darkness, against the spiritual forces of wickedness in the heavenly places"* (v. 12).

Are you appropriately dressed for the battle? Are your loins girded with truth, and have you put on the breastplate of righteousness? (v. 14) Are your feet shod with the Gospel of Peace? (v. 15) Are you protected by the shield of faith? (v. 16) Are you wearing the helmet of salvation and lifting the sword of the Spirit—which is the Word of God? (v. 17)

To be spiritually armed for the battle is the only way to resist the evil one. In order to be victorious, we must, *"be strong in the Lord and in the strength of His might"* (Ephesians 6:10).

We are in a war—and we can't afford to surrender. When boxer James Corbett was the heavyweight champion of the world, he was asked, "What is the most important thing a man must do to become a champion?"

Corbett responded, "Be willing to fight one more round!"

HE'S DEFEATED!

Satan is still stalking the earth, but you can rejoice in the fact that he is a defeated foe waiting for his final punishment. As Paul writes: *"The God of peace will soon crush Satan under your feet"* (Romans 16:20).

In his great revelation, John saw an angel coming down from Heaven to take hold of Satan, *"and he threw him into the abyss, and shut it and sealed it over him, so that he would not deceive the nations any longer"* (Revelation 20:3). The Bible assures us that the devil will be *"thrown into the lake of fire and...tormented day and night forever and ever"* (v. 10).

We can live in total victory because of the Blood of the Lamb and the word of our testimony (Revelation 12:11). That makes me shout "Hallelujah!"

"DELIVER US!"

Today, God gives us a choice. Will we serve the adversary or the Almighty?

As Jesus declares: *"No one can serve two masters; for either he will hate the one and love the other, or he will be devoted to one and despise the other"* (Matthew 6:24).

The next time you pray the Lord's Prayer, mean it from the depths of your soul when you say, *"Do not lead us into temptation, but deliver us from evil"* (Matthew 6:13). You can defeat Satan and experience God's Kingdom, power and glory *forever!*

TEN STEPS TO MAKING WISE CHOICES

In making our decisions,
we must use the brains God has given us.
But we must also use our heart—
which He has also given us.

FULTON OURSLER

A 270-pound man in New York recently sued four fast food restaurants for jeopardizing his health with their greasy, fatty fare. He claimed they were at fault for his two heart attacks: "They never warned me about the dangers of certain ingredients," the man complained on a network news show.

Isn't it amazing how people can't seem to take responsibility for their own actions? Smokers become concerned when their health suddenly fails. Yet on each and every pack of cigarettes the warning is very clearly printed: "SURGEON GENERAL'S WARNING: Smoking Causes Lung Cancer, Heart Disease, Emphysema, and May Complicate Pregnancy."

This may be difficult for some people to comprehend, but *you* are in control of what goes into your body. Regardless of the consequences, your choices are your responsibility!

Who makes the choice for you to take drugs? Does someone force you to eat high-cholesterol foods? Is someone holding a gun to your head when you cheat on your spouse? Are you being coerced into maxing out your credit cards?

Your present circumstances are the direct result of your personal decisions—not the choices someone else has made for you. Remember: God has gifted you with the power to choose, and He holds you responsible for how you use this power.

THE RIGHT PATH

There's a fascinating account in the Old Testament of when God spoke to a young prophet from Judah and sent him on a mission. The Lord told him, "This is where I want you to go. This is what I want you to do and say. And when you are finished, come straight back—don't eat bread or drink water or return the same way you came."

So the young man obeyed the Lord, accomplished his mission, and was on his way home when he met an old man who was one of the prophets of God living in Bethel. He invited the young man to *"Come home with me and eat bread"* (1 Kings 13:15). At first, the traveler refused the invitation, but the old man continued: *"I also am a prophet like you, and an angel spoke to me by the word of the Lord, saying, 'Bring him back with you to your house, that he may eat bread and drink water.' But he lied to him"* (v. 18).

The young man of God from Judah allowed himself to be deceived and—instead of obeying God's instructions— he chose to disobey. As a consequence of that unwise choice, he was devoured by a lion (v. 26). God had clearly told the young prophet the right path to take. However, he listened to the voice of a stranger and met an untimely death.

Don't allow other people to tell you something different from what you know God has spoken to you. Stay true to what God has said. Obey Him. Don't allow yourself to be deceived by strangers with false claims that they pretend are from God—or from anyone else, for that matter!

A SOUND STRATEGY

Today, the world has changed dramatically. We are bombarded with vast amounts of data, yet people continue to repeatedly make ill-advised choices. We have great knowledge, but not great wisdom. However, I believe there *is* a strategy for making sound, well-informed judgments day after day. Let me share 10 important steps to help you make wise choices.

1. Pray.

The scientists or philosophers who believe they have all the answers to life are only fooling themselves. Their mental powers, no matter how far developed, are as a grain of sand compared with the Creator's omnipotence. *"With Him are wisdom and might; To Him belong counsel and understanding"* (Job 12:13).

It is not enough to rely solely on logic, reason, or statistics. As Harry Truman once remarked, "How far would Moses have gone if he had taken a poll in Egypt?" We all desperately need the Lord's wisdom to guide us.

God knows you better than you know yourself. As the psalmist expresses:

> *O Lord, You have searched me and known me. You know when I sit down and when I rise up; You understand my thought from afar. You scrutinize my path and my lying down, and are intimately acquainted with all my ways. Even before there is a word on my tongue; behold, O Lord, You know it all* (Psalm 139:1-4).

Since God understands us so well, it only makes sense that we should ask for His direction in our lives. The Bible tells us: *"If any of you lacks wisdom, let him ask of God, who gives to all generously and without reproach, and it will be given to him"* (James 1:5). That's why we must spend time with Him in prayer.

2. Read the Word.

The ultimate source of wise decision-making is as close as your Bible. The psalmist asks: *"How can a young man keep his way pure? By keeping it according to Your word"* (Psalm 119:9).

Why choose to stumble in the dark? Ask God to brighten your journey: *"The unfolding of Your words gives light; It gives understanding to the simple"* (v. 130).

Yes, searching the Bible for direction is work, but it's well worth the effort. Go to God's Word and "dig out" His truths!

Too many Christians expect somebody else, such as their pastor, to "spoon feed" Scripture to them. Don't expect someone else to do your work for you! Go to the Word yourself, and discover what God is saying about the decisions you are facing.

The Word of God is filled with examples of choices people made—and the rewards and consequences they received as a result. Let their experience be your guide, and be certain your choices *always* line up with Scripture.

3. Sometimes, you need to fast.

Have you ever faced a challenge so monumental that you felt something in addition to prayer was needed? Something that would empower your prayers in the face of an overwhelming spiritual battle?

The disciples experienced this when they prayed for a little boy who had a demon—yet nothing happened. When Jesus arrived on the scene, He immediately rebuked the demon and it *"came out of him, and the boy was cured at once"* (Matthew 17:18).

The disciples came to Jesus privately and asked, *"Why could we not drive it out?"* (v. 19) Listen to the Lord's reply concerning casting out this stubborn demon: *"This kind does not go out except by prayer and fasting"* (v. 21).

What are the toughest decisions you are facing? Remember: Major problems require extraordinary solutions! God wants to address the issue by giving you a fervent passion to pray and to fast. Sometimes its not enough to pray; sometimes its not enough to go to the Word; sometimes you need to fast as well.

Fasting is a form of humbling yourself before God. When you humble yourself, God says He will exalt you. He'll give you the answer you need. Jesus Himself told us to fast (Matthew 6:16-17). Fasting is a spiritual exercise that overcomes your flesh, allowing God to give you fresh revelation. When you fast, God moves obstacles that prayer alone will not remove.

4. Offer God a sacrifice.

When you are prayerfully seeking the answer you need, give the Lord an offering that costs you something. I'm not talking about the ceremonies of the Old Testament that involved animal blood sacrifices and rites of purification. Since Jesus became our sacrifice for sin on the Cross, these observances are no longer necessary.

The words "living sacrifice" may sound like a contradiction, yet that's what God asks us to become (Romans 12:1). Give to the Lord *every* part of you as your living sacrifice to Him:

- Your hands—so that your touch brings glory to the Lord.

- Your feet—to walk as Jesus would walk.

- Your eyes—to see as God sees.

- Your ears—to hear what the Lord is saying.

- Your tongue—to speak what is pleasing to the Father.

- Your mind—to make Godly choices.

- Your heart—to have a compassion and love for others.

- Your time, talents and treasure—so that everything you are and have belongs to Him.

When you offer all that you are *completely* to the Lord, His decisions become yours.

5. Have a higher purpose.

If the options you are pursuing are purely for enhancing your image, building your reputation, or boosting your ego, you'd better think twice, especially if your actions are motivated by envy, jealousy, or revenge. God didn't place you on earth to be a superstar, or to "get even" with your enemies, but rather to have fellowship and communion with Him.

This is why before making a decision, you need to stop and ask yourself, "Will this choice bring honor and glory to the Lord?" As Paul wrote to the Believers at Colossae: *"Whatever you do in word or deed, do all in the name of the Lord Jesus, giving thanks through Him to God the Father"* (Colossians 3:17).

Never lose sight of the truth that God knows your every intention—and bases His rewards accordingly.

6. Weigh the alternatives.

Before blindly rushing ahead, ask yourself, "If I make this decision, what can I expect to take place?" Look at every possible scenario—the best that could happen AND the worst!

Look at the alternatives, and think about the consequences. Ask yourself...

- How will this decision affect those I love? *"He*

who troubles his own house will inherit the
wind, And the foolish will be servant to the
wisehearted" (Proverbs 11:29).

- Will this decision strengthen my spiritual life?
  The end result should be *"for the equipping of*
  the saints for the work of service, to the building
  up of the body of Christ" (Ephesians 4:12).

- Is this decision in God's will? *"Commit your works*
  to the Lord and your plans will be established"
  (Proverbs 16:3).

The ultimate consequences of your choices may not be
revealed until you stand before the Lord. The apostle Paul
prayed, *"that your love may abound still more and more in*
real knowledge and all discernment, so that you may approve
the things that are excellent, in order to be sincere and blame-
less until the day of Christ" (Philippians 1:9-10).

All of our choices need to be made with eternity in
view. Get those "scales" out. Weigh the alternatives carefully. What will be the consequence of making this choice
or not making it? What are the alternatives?

7. Think your decisions through.

I'm sure you have been in the presence of someone
whose mouth is in motion before his mind is in gear—
speaking before thinking! King Solomon had an opinion
about such a man: *"He who gives an answer before he*
hears; it is folly and shame to him" (Proverbs 18:13).

In the world of carpentry, there's a rule that says "measure twice and cut once." That is sound advice. Instead of
rushing into a hasty plan, take time to carefully weigh the
advantages and disadvantages.

Follow the example of the lowly ants, and do some

advance preparation. These small creatures decide in August what they'll be eating in January. *"Go to the ant, O sluggard, observe her ways and be wise, which, having no chief, officer or ruler, prepares her food in the summer and gathers her provision in the harvest"* (Proverbs 6:6-8).

You may wonder, "How can I plan ahead when I may need to make a lightning-fast judgment in a crisis? What if there is no time for analyzing the situation?"

Believe me when I tell you that reading and memorizing Scripture will give you the necessary tools to make instant choices. You will know how to fight the attacks of Satan, claim God's healing power, and connect with Heaven. In the words of the psalmist, *"Your word I have treasured in my heart, that I may not sin against You"* (Psalm 119:11). Also remember: *"Wise men store up knowledge, but with the mouth of the foolish, ruin is at hand"* (Proverbs 10:14).

Every time I am hit with a crisis—whether traveling in an airplane with a failed engine or facing a health emergency—out of my mouth begins to flow Scripture after Scripture. Often, I don't even remember having memorized the verses, yet I can quote them by heart. Backed by the Word and God's promises, I feel comfortable about making the necessary immediate decisions.

8. Seek Godly counsel.

I know it's human nature to think, "Look, I can do it by myself," yet you always need God's guidance and advice. Seeking help doesn't mean you are weak. In reality, it is a sign of strength!

In addition to finding direction, the Lord desires that we are spiritually accountable. If the great leaders of the Bible sought wisdom and help, why shouldn't you? Moses had his father-in-law, Jethro, while Paul turned to Barnabas and the elders of the Church.

Read the book of Proverbs and you'll understand what I mean. It has much to say concerning the need to seek Godly counsel:

- *"He who walks with wise men will be wise, but the companion of fools will suffer harm"* (Proverbs 13:20).

- *"For by wise guidance you will wage war, and in abundance of counselors there is victory"* (Proverbs 24:6).

- *"Listen to counsel and accept discipline, that you may be wise the rest of your days"* (Proverbs 19:20).

- *"Without consultation, plans are frustrated, but with many counselors they succeed"* (Proverbs 15:22).

Don't blindly accept every offer of advice at face value, or you may wind up receiving counsel from the devil himself. Be on the alert for wolves in sheep's clothing. Speaking with His disciples on the Mount of Olives, Jesus warned: *"If anyone says to you, 'Behold, here is the Christ,' or 'There He is,' do not believe him. For false Christs and false prophets will arise and will show great signs and wonders, so as to mislead, if possible, even the elect"* (Matthew 24:23-24).

There's no need to announce your problems to the whole world. Be discrete. This is why you need to choose a trusted counselor who will keep what you say in total confidence.

Before you allow someone to speak into your life, know the background of the individual. Find a Believer who is grounded in the Word and lives a blameless life. Specifically, look for a person who has experienced what you are now facing. It's always encouraging to listen to someone who has "been there" and, with God's help, has emerged victorious.

Remember: Godly counsel—if it's truly from God—is going to confirm something that God's already spoken to you. Godly counsel always lines up with the Word of God. He *never* goes against His Word.

After being married for over 35 years, I've also learned that before making a major decision, I should talk the situation over with Barbara. Her input on the issue is more than vital—it's Scriptural. The Lord asks: *"Can two walk together, except they be agreed?"* (Amos 3:3 KJV)

Perhaps the Lord has given you a vision for the future, and you need to talk with someone who has already reached a similar goal. The advice you receive may allow you to avoid dangerous pitfalls. However, let me offer this word of caution to you: Never rely on man more than you rely on God. If the Lord has revealed something to you directly—either through His clear voice or through the Word—act on that divine directive first. After all, *"There is no wisdom and no understanding, and no counsel against the Lord"* (Proverbs 21:30). When you believe you've already heard from God, the counselor's role is to confirm what the Lord has told you.

9. Be led by peace.

People have asked: "David, how do you truly know you've made the right decision?" I love to answer, "Because I have a peace about it!" To me, that's the primary way the Lord confirms His will and His Word.

When God's peace rules, the Lord becomes like an

umpire, resolving issues and letting you know what is right. I love the words of Paul as written in the Amplified Bible: *"Let the peace from Christ rule (act as an umpire continually) in your hearts [deciding and settling with finality all questions that arise in your minds, in that peaceful state] to which as [members of Christ's] one body you were called [to live]"* (Colossians 3:15).

Also, when you make a decision contrary to God's will, you will know it. There will be a restlessness—an uneasy feeling in the pit of your stomach. That's the Lord telling you to put things on hold, perhaps even to back up and to reverse the choice you have made. I've observed those who make choices out of disobedience or rebellion. They balk and insist, "I'm not going to do that." But when a decision is made out of a pure heart and a desire to please the Lord, I believe He will honor you.

If your decision is the wrong one but has been made out of the integrity of your heart, you can go to God and say, "Lord, I took this step because I believed it was what You wanted me to do. Now I'm asking You to help me in this situation—to lead me to the place You need me to be." Before long, the Lord will open new doors or perhaps bring some*one* or some*thing* into your life to steer you back to the right path.

When in doubt, go back to the Lord's peace. Return to the moment when you first felt God speak to you. What was it that caused your heart to feel His comfort and assurance? Make a U-turn and recapture that peace before you proceed any further.

Pray that *"the peace of God, which surpasses all comprehension, will guard your hearts and your minds in Christ Jesus"* (Philippians 4:7).

Don't move in one direction or another. Don't make a

choice until you have peace again in your spirit. Don't move. Don't move forward. Don't move backwards. Don't move to the left. Don't move to the right. Don't move, *period,* until God gives you peace in your spirit.

10. Stay committed to your decision.

Once you make a choice, be determined to see it through unless and until God gives you some other specific direction. The world will encourage you to have a backup strategy—just in case your first plan doesn't work. With God's guidance in your life, there is no need for a "Plan B."

When you know what the Lord has specifically told you, but it hasn't come to pass, examine your steps to see if you took a wrong turn somewhere. Never blame God. Instead, ask His forgiveness if you weren't persistent and faithful to His plan.

Accept what the Lord tells you and don't be tempted to vacillate. The Bible cautions: *"The one who doubts is like the surf of the sea, driven and tossed by the wind. For that man ought not to expect that he will receive anything from the Lord, being a double-minded man, unstable in all his ways"* (James 1:6-8).

Everyone goes through tough times, and you will be challenged regarding your choices. Expect it! Jesus says: *"In the world you have tribulation, but take courage; I have overcome the world"* (John 16:33).

If the Lord Jesus has emerged victorious, then as His child—so will you!

SHE WOULDN'T LEAVE

There's power in persistence! In our prayers, we should

become like the woman who came to Elisha when her son was dying. When she reached the man of God, she grabbed his feet and wouldn't let go!

The prophet tried to have his servant, Gehazi, go to the dying boy and lay Elisha's wooden staff on the child's face. Still, the woman insisted, boldly announcing: *"As the Lord lives and as you yourself live, I will not leave you"* (2 Kings 4:30).

So the prophet walked with the woman to her house and saw the boy lying dead on his couch. Elisha went in to him, shut the door, and began calling on God.

The Bible records that *"he went up and lay on the child, and put his mouth on his mouth and his eyes on his eyes and his hands on his hands, and he stretched himself on him; and the flesh of the child became warm"* (2 Kings 4:34).

Suddenly, the boy sneezed seven times and opened his eyes. He was completely healed! The mother's persistence led to a miracle!

DON'T LOSE HEART!

Jesus tells the story of a judge who cared little about the people he served. In that same town lived a widow who kept coming to him with the same plea: *"Grant me justice against my adversary"* (Luke 18:3).

For quite a while, the judge couldn't be bothered and refused to help her. But finally, he said to himself, *"Even though I do not fear God nor respect man, yet because this widow bothers me, I will give her legal protection, otherwise by continually coming she will wear me out"* (vs. 4-5).

Why did Jesus share this parable with His disciples? It was to tell them to be as persistent as the widow and *"that at all times they ought to pray and not to lose heart"* (v. 1).

When you have followed God's principles for making wise choices, step out in faith and be decisive. You'll be amazed at what takes place when you choose to walk in God's assurance and act on His authority.

11

DETERMINE YOUR ETERNAL DESTINY

*When ten thousand, times
ten thousand, times
ten thousand years have passed,
eternity will have just begun.*

BILLY SUNDAY

Once I heard about a gardener working for a large estate in northern Italy who was giving a visitor a tour of the beautifully manicured grounds. Just before the tourist left, he said, "Let me commend you for the fantastic way you keep up the property. It's perfect!" Then he asked, "By the way, when was the last time the owner was here?"

The gardener paused for a moment and replied, "It was about ten years ago."

Surprised at the answer, the visitor asked, "Then why do you keep these gardens in such immaculate condition?"

"Because I'm expecting him to return," responded the groundskeeper.

The visitor continued, "Is he coming next week?"

The gardener shrugged his shoulders and answered, "I don't know exactly when he is coming, but it could be today." Instead of looking down the road, impatiently waiting for his master's return, the gardener was busy at his work, trimming the hedges and planting flowers.

My friend, we are about to experience the soon return of *our* Master—and the day is closer than we can imagine. The Lord declares: *"Behold, I am coming quickly, and My reward is with Me, to render to every man according to what he has done"* (Revelation 22:12).

You may respond, "Wait a minute! That sounds as though the 'reward' could be amazing or awful, depending on how we live on earth." This is exactly true.

In His parable concerning the sheep and the goats, Jesus explains what is going to occur. He says, *"When the Son of Man comes in His glory, and all the angels with Him, then He will sit on His glorious throne. All the nations will be gathered before Him; and He will separate them from one another, as the shepherd separates the sheep from the goats"* (Matthew 25:31-32).

Jesus continues, *"and He will put the sheep on His right, and the goats on the left. Then the King will say to those on His right, 'Come, you who are blessed of My Father, inherit the kingdom prepared for you from the foundation of the world'"* (vs. 33-34).

Eternal existence is waiting for *every* person, whether in Heaven or in hell: *"These* [speaking of those who did not serve the Lord] *will go away into eternal punishment, but the righteous into eternal life"* (v. 46).

YOU WILL BE REPAID

When Jesus was invited to eat at the home of a prominent man, He asked His host to give a banquet and invite the poor, the crippled, the lame and the blind, *"and you will be blessed, since they do not have the means to repay you; for you will be repaid at the resurrection of the righteous"* (Luke 14:14).

The word Jesus used for "repaid" is *apodidomai—apo* meaning "back" and *didomai* meaning "to give." The Lord was telling the man, "For what you give, you will be given back."

It's the same word Jesus used in telling the story of the Good Samaritan: *"When I return I will repay you"* (Luke 10:35). And Jesus tells us, *"Whoever gives you a cup of water to drink because of your name as followers of Christ, truly I say to you, he will not lose his reward"* (Mark 9:41).

Payday is coming! One day soon, we *all* will stand in the presence of God, and He will reward us for the choices we have made and the actions we have taken here on earth.

WHAT ABOUT DEEDS?

Let me remind you again that your choices not only determine *where* you will spend eternity, but also *how.*

Many Believers aren't concerned about what awaits them "on the other side"—their primary concern is knowing that they are *going* to Heaven. But they'll be surprised when they stand before God and realize their rewards are not based simply on salvation.

Remember: Jesus has already paid that price for you, and your faith in Him gains you entry into Heaven. Once there, you will be judged based on what you did as a Believer: your works and the Seeds you have Sown. Yes, every man will be repaid *"according to his deeds"* (Matthew 16:27).

To put it as simply as I know how, your eternal destination is based on your belief—and your actions based on your beliefs. For example, God's Word says, *"If you confess* [action] *with your mouth Jesus as Lord, and believe* [belief] *in your heart that God raised Him from the dead, you will be saved; for with the heart a person believes, resulting in righteousness, and with the mouth he confesses, resulting in salvation"* (Romans 10:9-10).

The consequences of this decision will determine *where* you will spend your everlasting future. The other choices you make in life—including your behavior—unlock the door to Heaven's rewards and determine *how* you will spend eternity. Your actions in this life have a direct bearing on what Heaven will be like for you.

THE SECRET OF ABUNDANCE

The Almighty is also going to judge us based on the spiritual light we possess (Luke 12:48). He will ask us, "What was the motivation of your heart? What did you do with your talents and abilities?"

Jesus told the story of a man who was going on a journey. Before leaving, he called his servants and entrusted his property to them—giving each one different amounts of talents (money). The servant who received five talents put the money to work and gained five more. The one with two talents gained two more. But the man who received just one talent dug a hole in the ground and hid his master's money.

After a long time, the owner returned home. When he learned what the first two servants had accomplished, he exclaimed to each, *"Well done, good and faithful slave. You were faithful with a few things, I will put you in charge of many things; enter into the joy of your master"* (Matthew 25:23).

However, the servant who was afraid and hid his talent was admonished: *"You wicked, lazy slave...you ought to have put my money in the bank, and on my arrival I would have received my money back with interest"* (Matthew 25:27). Then he took the hidden talent and gave it to the servant who already had *ten* talents.

Through this parable, Jesus teaches this important lesson: *"To everyone who has, more shall be given, and he will have an abundance; but from the one who does not have, even what he does have shall be taken away. Throw out the worthless slave into the outer darkness; in that place there will be weeping and gnashing of teeth"* (vs. 29-30).

THE ULTIMATE REWARD

I hope you realize how close we are to the Second Coming of Christ. The Bible tells us what is about to take place: *"The Lord Himself will descend from heaven with a shout, with the voice of the archangel and with the trumpet of God, and the dead in Christ will rise first, then we who are alive and remain will be caught up together with them in the clouds to meet the Lord in the air, and so we shall always be with the Lord"* (1 Thessalonians 4:16-17).

Even as I write these words, God is putting the finishing touches on your reward. Jesus says, *"If I go and prepare a place for you, I will come again and receive you to Myself, that where I am, there you may be also"* (John 14:3).

Heaven—mentioned 632 times in the Bible—is going to be a reward beyond anything our earthly minds can imagine. I remember hearing about a little girl who was taking an evening walk with her father. She looked up at the stars and exclaimed, "Oh, Daddy, if the wrong side of Heaven is so beautiful, what must the right side be like!"

The Bible tells us *"Things which eye has not seen and ear has not heard, and which have not entered the heart of man, all that God has prepared for those who love Him"* (1 Corinthians 2:9).

What a place Heaven will be! Every tear will be wiped from our eyes *"and there will no longer be any death; there will no longer be any mourning, or crying, or pain; the first things have passed away"* (Revelation 21:4).

Just think what you're about to experience! You will...
...eat of the tree of life (Revelation 2:7).
...receive hidden manna (v. 17).
...be arrayed in white garments (Revelation 3:5).
...have your name written in the Book of Life (v. 5).

...have your name confessed by Christ before the
Father (v. 5).
...be a pillar in the Temple of God (v. 12).
...sit with Christ on His throne (v. 21).

WHAT—AND *WHERE*—ARE YOU SOWING?

Specifically, what are you choosing to do today that
will prepare you for God's great tomorrow? When you
invest in something bigger than yourself, you will receive
a greater reward.

That's why I encourage you to Sow into Good Ground.
In Matthew 13 the Bible describes different levels of
Harvests—some thirty, some sixty, some one hundred
fold. It's sad to say, but not every church or ministry is
Good Ground. Some churches and ministries will yield
only a thirty or sixty-fold increase.

I encourage you to invest your Seed where it will bring
the greatest return for the Kingdom of God.

12

THE CHOICE
IS YOURS

A human being
is a deciding being.

VIKTOR E. FRANKL

In Genesis 1:26, God said, *"Let Us make man in Our image, according to Our likeness."* Yet I don't believe our creation in the image of God has anything to do with our physical features. Instead, God's image means we have the power of *choice.*

The Lord didn't create us to be like robots or like puppets on a string. We're not designed to worship or draw near to Him because He pulls some kind of cosmic string that makes us do so. It's a matter of choice.

The freedom to choose is a precious gift. Throughout our life, God sets choices before us. Although The Lord gladly reveals His will, we have the power to make our own decisions.

This means that if we love God, worship Him, praise Him, seek Him, and take time to be in His presence, it's because we've *chosen* to—not because there's some kind of mystical, unseen hand that has forced our compliance.

After all, no one wants a forced love affair.

Because God created you with the ability to seek Him, you can have as close of a relationship with Him as you would like. Every day, you can experience as much of His presence as you want.

So ask yourself today, how intimate of a relationship with God would you like to have? The choice is yours. You can experience as much or as little of God as you choose.

Do you want to just know *about* the Lord? Are you content to just be His casual acquaintance? Or are you intent on drawing near to Him, discovering a place of true friendship and intimacy?

AN INVESTMENT OF TIME

Your Heavenly Father longs for an intimate personal

relationship with you. But intimate relationships take time. You can't possibly have an intimate relationship with someone you only see or talk to once a year, once a month, or even once a week. Relationships develop as a result of deliberately choosing to spend time together.

Every day, you face a choice about your relationship with your Heavenly Father. What kind of a relationship do you want with Him? Do you hunger for ever-deepening intimacy with Him?

Today, I pray you will make a commitment to spend daily time with the Lord. Time in His Word...time in prayer...time in worship...time alone with Him. He will nourish you on "daily bread" as you bask in His presence.

Friend, I believe you are at a crossroads. God is setting before you a life of incredible blessing and abundance. But the choice is yours.

THREE KEY SCRIPTURES

I want to deposit three Scriptures into your spirit as we close.

First, Deuteronomy 11:26-28: *"Behold, I set before you this day a choice, a blessing and a curse. A blessing if you obey the commandments of the Lord, your God, which I command you this day and a curse if you will not obey the commandments of the Lord but turn aside out of the way that I have commanded you this day."*

Second, Jeremiah 21:8: *"You shall also say to this people, 'Thus says the Lord, "Behold, I set before you the way of life and the way of death."'"*

Third, Deuteronomy 30:19-20: *"I call heaven and earth to record this day against you, that I have set before you life and death, blessing and cursing: therefore choose life, that both you and your seed may live: That you would love the Lord your God, and that you would obey his voice, and that you would cleave unto him: for he is your life, and the length of your days."*

Earlier in this book, I shared how the Lord was impressing upon me that there were three kinds of people who needed the message contained within these pages. I don't know what kind of choices you're facing today or what category you're in. You may be one who is about to make a terrible choice that you're going to regret forever. You may be one who is about to make one of the greatest choices you could ever imagine. Or you may be one who is sitting in the land of indecision.

I challenge you today to choose wisely—choose *LIFE*— choose obedience. If you want to change your future, you must change your choices. Your future is shaped by the choices you make in this life, and the rewards you will receive in Heaven are going to be based on the *deposits* you made *there* from the *choices* you made *here*. Choose wisely.

Barbara and I want to pray with you and for you today. We want to agree in prayer with you that God will help you make the right choices—choices that will bring great rewards now in this lifetime AND in the world to come.

IT'S TIME TO PRAY

Let's pray together:

> *Father, we come together before you in the name of Jesus. Thank You for Your Word and that You have set before us life and death, blessings and curses. Thank You that You desire for us to choose wisely so that You can reward us with Your good gifts.*

Speak to us through Your Word in our times of prayer. Speak to us through Godly counsel.

May we hear Your voice clearly as we humble ourselves through fasting before You. Speak clearly to us and help us to know the best way to take.

Father, for those who are on the brink of making a critically wrong choice at this moment, whoever they are, wherever they might be, we pray in Jesus' name that they will stop. Help them, Lord, to look to You for Your help and the wisdom to make the right decision. As difficult as it may be for them to obey You, give them the strength to choose wisely.

Lord, for those who are on the verge of making some of the greatest choices they'll ever make in their life, let Your rewards be theirs, in this life and in the world to come.

Father, help all of our choices to be like gold, silver, and precious stones. Don't let our choices be those that will burn up as hay, wood, and stubble. Help us not to suffer loss by making wrong choices.

Lord, for those who are in the valley of indecision and doubt, I pray You will move them by the power of Your Holy Spirit to make right, wise, and obedient choices. Take away their fear and give them faith. Replace their doubt and despair with courage and hope.

Help us, Father, to choose wisely how we Sow our time, our talent, and our treasure, since Your rewards for obedience are beyond measure. Help us to choose wisely. In Jesus' name. Amen.

GOD'S GREAT PLAN FOR YOU

My friend, I want to assure you that God has a marvelous plan for your life—and He offers to show you the right choices that He is asking you to make. This is why I encourage you to trust in the Lord with all your heart and let Him direct your path (Proverbs 3:5-6).

As you face these vital decisions, please know that Barbara and I and the prayer ministers of Inspiration Ministries are praying that you will make your decisions according to the Father's will—choices that will fulfill His purpose for you.

During those troublesome times when you feel you've taken a wrong path, simply stop and say: "Lord, I'm sorry. I am asking you to bring me back to the place I need to be. Lead me into your perfect plan."

We are praying and believing together with you that the choices you make will bring God's great rewards—that His best will be performed in your life, now, and in the life to come. Remember:

We Are Here for You!

SCRIPTURES
FOR

BETTER CHOICES
AND A
BETTER LIFE

Life is a series of daily decisions. We constantly ask ourselves, "Should I open this door or leave it closed? Should I take the path to the right or travel the road that goes left?"

In this book, we examined how choices affect our relationships, our reputation, our riches, and our righteousness. However, the most important question we should ask is, "What does God's Word say about my choices?"

I encourage you to open your Bible and discover what happens as the result of your decisions. Take the time to read these Scriptures in their context and apply them to your life.

YOUR WISE CHOICE:

When you choose to believe in Christ as your Savior...

YOUR REWARD:

You will spend eternity with Him (1 John 5:13).

or

YOUR UNWISE CHOICE:

When you choose to be stubborn and unrepentant...

YOUR CONSEQUENCE:

You are storing up wrath and God's judgment for yourself (Romans 2:5).

YOUR WISE CHOICE:

When you choose to Sow bountifully...

YOUR REWARD:

You will Reap bountifully (2 Corinthians 9:6).

or

YOUR UNWISE CHOICE:

When you choose to Sow sparingly...

YOUR CONSEQUENCE:

You will Reap sparingly (2 Corinthians 9:6).

YOUR WISE CHOICE:

When you choose to repent and ask God's forgiveness...

YOUR REWARD:

He will hear and answer you (Isaiah 1:15-16).

or

YOUR UNWISE CHOICE:

When you choose to live in sin...

YOUR CONSEQUENCE:

Your prayers are not answered, and poverty comes (1 Kings 8:33-35).

YOUR WISE CHOICE:

When you choose to spend time in God's presence...

YOUR REWARD:

He will bless you with peace and abundance (1 Chronicles 13:14).

or

YOUR UNWISE CHOICE:

When you place your faith in others instead of the Lord...

YOUR CONSEQUENCE:
You will receive God's judgment (2 Kings 1:3-4).

YOUR WISE CHOICE:
When you choose to Sow good Seeds into your children...
YOUR REWARD:
They will receive a lifetime of blessing
(1 Chronicles 22:12-13).
or
YOUR UNWISE CHOICE:
When you choose to live in disobedience...
YOUR CONSEQUENCE:
It can affect your descendants for many generations
(2 Kings 5:27).

YOUR WISE CHOICE:
When you choose to return to the Lord...
YOUR REWARD:
You will find compassion, grace and forgiveness
(2 Chronicles 30:9).
or
YOUR UNWISE CHOICE:
When you choose to become friends with the wicked...
YOUR CONSEQUENCE:
God's wrath will fall upon you (2 Chronicles 19:2).

YOUR WISE CHOICE:

When you choose to humble yourself before the Lord...

YOUR REWARD:

He will hear your prayer (2 Chronicles 34:27).

or

YOUR UNWISE CHOICE:

When you choose to be proud...

YOUR CONSEQUENCE:

God will resist you (1 Peter 4:6).

YOUR WISE CHOICE:

When you choose to love the Lord...

YOUR REWARD:

He will deliver you and set you on high (Psalm 91:14).

or

YOUR UNWISE CHOICE:

When you choose to make an alliance that is not of God...

YOUR CONSEQUENCE:

You will receive shame and humiliation (Isaiah 30:1-3).

YOUR WISE CHOICE:

When you choose to acquire God's wisdom and understanding...

YOUR REWARD:

He will exalt you (Proverbs 4:7).

or
YOUR UNWISE CHOICE:
When you choose to neglect God's counsel and refuse His correction...
YOUR CONSEQUENCE:
You will eat the fruit of your own ways.
(Proverbs 1:24-26).

YOUR WISE CHOICE:
When you choose to trust in the Lord with all your heart and acknowledge Him in all your ways...
YOUR REWARD:
He will make your paths straight (Proverbs 3:5-6).
or
YOUR UNWISE CHOICE:
When you choose to walk according to the stubbornness of your own heart...
YOUR CONSEQUENCE:
The Lord will declare calamity against you (Jeremiah 16:10-12).

YOUR WISE CHOICE:
When you choose to honor the Lord with the first and best of what you have...
YOUR REWARD:
You will always have plenty (Proverbs 3:9).
or
YOUR UNWISE CHOICE:
When you choose to give the Lord your second best...

YOUR CONSEQUENCE:

He is not pleased and does not accept your offering (Malachi 1:6-10).

YOUR WISE CHOICE:

When you choose to give attention to the Lord and refuse to be enticed with the things of this world...

YOUR REWARD:

All your ways will be established (Proverbs 4:20-27).

or

YOUR UNWISE CHOICE:

When you choose to gain the whole world and forfeit your soul...

YOUR CONSEQUENCE:

It will profit you nothing (Matthew 16:26).

YOUR WISE CHOICE:

When you choose to place your hope and trust in the Lord...

YOUR REWARD:

You will become as a tree planted by the water (Jeremiah 7:7-8).

or

YOUR UNWISE CHOICE:

When you choose to turn from God and trust in your own strength...

YOUR CONSEQUENCE:
You will inhabit the wilderness (Jeremiah 17:5-6).

YOUR WISE CHOICE:
When you choose to Sow your tithes and offerings into the storehouse of God...
YOUR REWARD:
He will open the windows of Heaven and pour out a blessing you cannot contain (Malachi 3:10).
or
YOUR UNWISE CHOICE:
When you choose to rob God of your tithes and offerings...
YOUR CONSEQUENCE:
You are cursed with a curse (Malachi 3:8-9).

Your Creator and loving Heavenly Father couldn't have made it any more clear. For every choice you make, there is a certain reward or consequence.

What God declared to the children of Israel, He is also saying to you: *"I have set before you life and death, the blessing and the curse. So **choose life** in order that you may live, you and your descendants, by loving the Lord your God, by obeying His voice, and by holding fast to Him; for this is your life and the length of your days"* (Deuteronomy 30:19-20).

THE CHOICE IS *YOURS!*

ABOUT THE AUTHOR

DAVID CERULLO, with a strong business background and a passion for ministry, has a vision to impact people for Christ worldwide through media.

He and his wife, Barbara, have established Inspiration Ministries, an international media ministry based at the City of Light in South Carolina. Over 150 nations are being reached with the Gospel of Jesus Christ through Inspiration TV.

Having achieved national and international recognition as a television broadcaster and religious leader, David is a member of the National Cable Television Association, the Cable and Telecommunications Association for Marketing, the National Association of Television Program Executives, and has served on the Board of Directors for the National Religious Broadcasters Association.

David and Barbara have been married for more than 35 years and have two adult children and five grandchildren.

Visit their website at **inspiration.org** to receive teachings from God's Word, ministry updates, or to request prayer.

God Answers Prayer!

"If two of you agree on earth concerning anything that they ask, it will be done for them by My Father in Heaven."
— MATTHEW 18:19

"Thanks so much for your prayers for my husband Michael, who had been diagnosed with cancer. Michael went back for a checkup, and the doctor said his cancer is GONE! Praise the Lord!" — HELEN

"Your prayers and those of our friends have brought Divine healing to my mom's thyroid disease! She's returned to her former health!" — JAMES

"My wife's back was healed when your prayer minister agreed with me in prayer!" — ALLEN

"Thank you for your prayers! I've received a total healing regarding high blood pressure and a possible stroke." — IBIRONKE

Our prayer ministers welcome the opportunity to agree together with you in prayer and believe God to step into the circumstances of your life with His supernatural power!

Visit inspiration.org/prayer or call:

US: 803-578-1800   **Intl: +800 9982 4677**
UK: 0845 683 0584   **Caribbean: (877) 487-7782**

"Thank you for having one of your prayer ministers call and pray with me today. The call came at just the right time, and it made me feel like someone really cares. Again, thank you for the call just to pray with me." — GLORIA

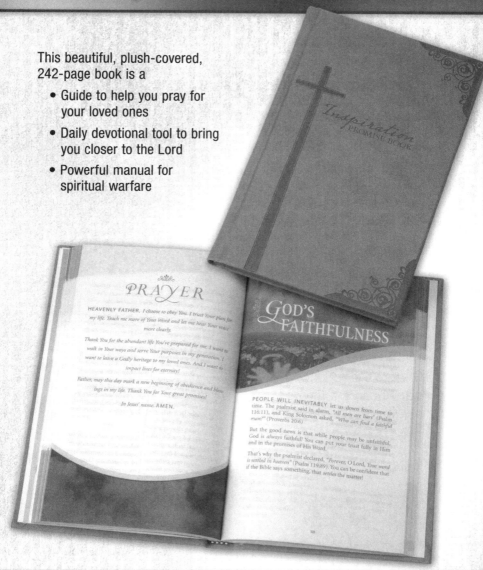

Do You Need a MIRACLE from God?

God Is a God of MIRACLES!

Do you need God's supernatural intervention today in your...

- **BODY, SOUL, OR SPIRIT?**
- **FINANCES, HOME, OR JOB?**
- **RELATIONSHIPS WITH LOVED ONES?**

This life-changing ministry resource will help you experience the miracle you need from Him!

Get ready to receive YOUR miracle!

"How to Receive Your Miracle tells me how to look forward to God's promises for complete healing in my life. This book has been an eye opener for me to the keys of living!" — KAREN

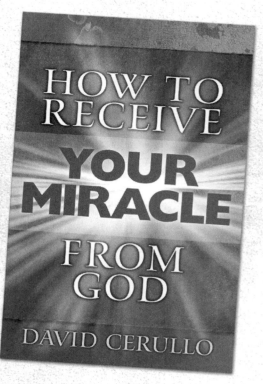

Hope For *Your* New Beginning

God wants to step into the circumstances of your life with His supernatural breakthroughs!

If you need a New Beginning in your...

Marriage • Job
Health • Finances
Children

...Hope For Your New Beginning book and audio CD will provide the tools you need to experience victory and abundance in Christ.

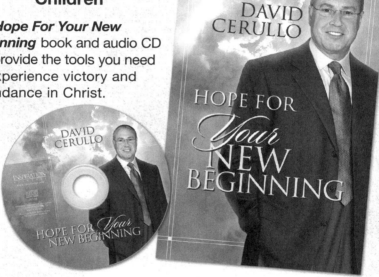

*"I was blessed by your **New Beginnings** book. This is such a profound word from the heart of God, and I have asked the Lord to order my steps into His new beginning. I want all the miracles and new beginnings He has ordained for me and for my family in the years to come."* — INGRID

Are YOU Ready for **BATTLE?**

"BATTLE FOR YOUR LIFE"
Will Give You the Tools You Need to Triumph Over the Enemy!

This timely manual will equip you to pull down enemy strongholds so you can discover God's destiny for your life!

The war is real. The enemy is real. His power is real. His agenda to steal, kill, and destroy is real.

You don't need to be a victim!

BATTLE FOR YOUR LIFE will give you the vital keys you need for victorious spiritual warfare in your life.

"I have read your book, Battle for Your Life, and I see now where Satan has almost destroyed me and my family. But I'm fighting back now that I realize a real spiritual evil is assaulting my children and me and my job. Thanks and God bless you!"

— HUGH

Visit inspiration.org/gifts or call Partner Services t◄ ministry tools as a "Thank You" gift for partnering

Partner Services — US: 803-578-1899 • UK: 0845 683 058◄

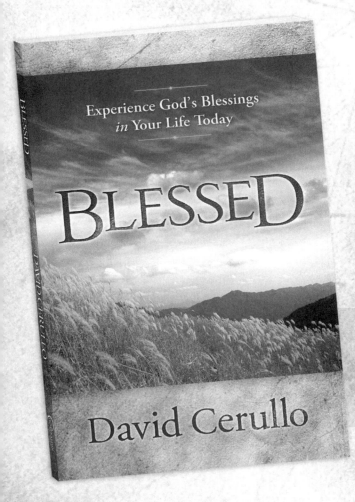

God wants to give you the breakthrough you need!

ANCIENT SECRETS OF THE TABERNACLE REVEALED

This book was written for those who truly want a deeper relationship with God that will take them past head knowledge into an experience of intimacy, power, and transformation.

THE ANGELS IN HEAVEN REJOICE

You will not only begin to experience the fullness of your new faith and grow in your personal relationship with Jesus, but you will also learn what it means to be a "Christ-follower"—with all of the joy, promises, and responsibilities of serving your Lord.

WHERE DO PEOPLE GO WHEN THEY DIE?

Have you ever wondered if there is life after death, if there is really a Heaven and hell, or whether science can confirm the testimonies of people who've returned from the dead?

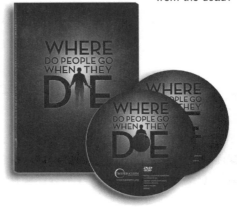

HEAL ME O LORD!

If this is the cry of your heart today – either for yourself or a loved one – this package will reveal proven Scriptural keys to unleash God's healing power!

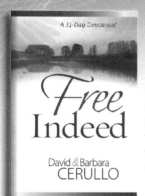
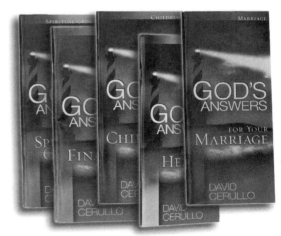

We Are Here for *You*

On Our Website 24/7/365!

Visit us online today at inspiration.org!

- Daily Devotionals
- Opportunities to Give
- Prayer Ministry
- Video Streaming
- Ministry Updates
- Thrilling Testimonies
- Inspirational Tools
- Encouraging Articles

And more!

This is just one more way we're blessing and impacting people for Christ worldwide... starting with you!